BREAKING THROUGH THE WALL

BREAKING
THROUGH THE WALL
A MARATHONER'S STORY

Dear Frieda,
You're wonderful.
I love your
spirit
We're strong women

DOLORES E. CROSS

THIRD WORLD PRESS CHICAGO

Third World Press
Publishers since 1967

Printed in the United States of America

04 03 02 01 00 5 4 3 2 1

Cover design by Nicole M. Mitchell

Library of Congress Cataloging-in-Publication Data

Cross, Dolores E.
   Breaking through the wall: a marathoner's story /Dolores E. Cross
p.cm.
   ISBN: 0-88378-165-4 (alk. paper)—ISBN 0-88378-166-2 (pbk.: alk. paper)
   1. Cross, Dolores E. 2. Afro-American women--Biography. 3.
   Afro-Americans--Biography. 4. Afro-American college presidents--
   Biography 5. Marathon running--United States--Biography. 6.
   Successful people--United States--Biography. 7. Afro-Americans--
   Conduct of life. I. Title.

E185.97.C85 C76 2000
796.42'52'092—dc21
[B]   99-052640

To my mother, who tried to break through the wall
again and again.

CONTENTS

PREFACE

This book is about breaking through the wall. About going the distance. About refusing to be constrained by words and attitudes about race, gender and age that attempt to deny your humanity and birthright to achieve.

I am a veteran marathoner, both literally and figuratively. A marathon is 26.2 miles of challenges. Running that long and that far uncovers your soul. Running that far and that long reveals what you've done to build your base, what you've learned about your body, mind and spirit.

Marathoners speak with dread of hitting the wall. The wall looms before you at just about mile 20, sometimes before and sometimes after. The body, mind and spirit come to what feels like a running in place, a great yawning pause, a frustrating inertia as you want to move on. There are many ways to explain the halt: lactic acid in the muscles, dehydration, inadequate carbohydrates the night before. Simply put, you don't have a base from which to draw energy to take you farther. Despite your wants and your passions, you just can't do it.

Long before I, as a 50-year-old, ran the first of my 18 literal marathons, I looked with dread at hitting the wall and padding weakly to a breathless stop. I felt the brutal assumptions and labels used to make me invisible or discourage me from going on. The racism, sexism and ageism I encountered were meant to make me think I didn't have the base from which to draw, the energy to go on. But the naysayers were wrong.

Being 50 doesn't mean you cannot run a marathon. Being black, first-generation college-educated and female doesn't mean you cannot—should not—aspire to be all you can be. It does not mean that you cannot act boldly and stand for something.

Being in your 60s does not mean that you can no longer play a major role in raising the local, state and national consciousness of what can be done to help students of all ages, races, ethnic backgrounds and levels of preparedness succeed.

You just have to keep going. You have to break through the wall—again and again.

ACKNOWLEDGMENTS

When you write a book about your life, you find yourself not only wanting to thank people for helping you with the book, but also for their place in your life. The thanks here are double.

I want to thank my mother, Ozie Johnson Tucker. In March 1993, she visited me in Chicago and spent many hours at my desk at home, writing in longhand. When she returned to New Jersey, she left behind pages on the story of her life. She wrote about her joy in raising two daughters and living to enjoy her five grandchildren. Her words made me thirst to know more about her journey—and to begin to put my own on paper.

Thank you to my children, Jane Cross and Thomas Cross Jr., for their patience, love and support as I changed course, moved ahead and often left them to ponder, "What's Mom up to now?"

Thank you to my sister Jean Dale Tucker McRae, who worried that I would say too much in the book. Yet as the book proceeded, she worried that I couldn't capture it all. You're right, Jean!

Special thanks to Renee Williams, who listened, interviewed friends and family, wrote and shared what she had heard and started me on my way with early drafts and coaching, "This has got to be your book."

Thank you to Kelley Fead who pored over diary entries and jottings in various forms, editing the manuscript and advising me so often, "Enough already or we'll never get a book out."

Thank you to Gwendolyn Mitchell of Third World Press

who offered a steady hand and eased my worries that my voice would be lost.

Thanks to Barbara McAdoo, Marva Jolly, Joyce Ann Joyce and Marcia Cross who frequently asked, "Where's the book? How's it coming along?" And to Barry Hastings, who gave me the encouraging word of "wonderful" after reading the first 100 pages.

Thank you to Kathleen Spivack who during a summer writer's retreat in Burgundy, France, encouraged me to write a short piece on running my first marathon and Caroline Dunston who provided a cottage in Rio Caliente, Mexico, for me to complete the first draft. Thanks to Gayle Manning for her help closer to the end of the process. And thanks to Dennis Cabral and Susan Lourenco Williams for their coaching in difficult times.

Thanks to the following other family members whom you meet in the book:

My father, Charles Tucker; my brother-in-law Clinton (Jake McRae); his and Jean's children, Karen, Steven and Tina; my cousin Harry Winston; my paternal grandmother and grandfather, Mary Winston Tucker and the Rev. Thomas T. Tucker; my maternal grandmother and grandfather, Melissa Johnson and Haywood Johnson; my aunt and uncles on the Tucker side, Carolyn and Harrison with children Ronald and David, Samuel and Eugenia (Jean), Carlton, Roger and Ruth, Matthew and Edith, and Frank and Dorothy, with children Lillian and Francine; my aunts and uncles on the Johnson side, Lottie, Lona and Willie, Minnie and Willie Edward, Lucy and Noah, Monroe and Roy; the father of my children and my former husband Thomas E. Cross and his cousins Steve, Carolyn, Alice and Paul Murphy with children Karann, Pat, Allie and my goddaughter Jeanne.

And I thank the family members not included here by name as well—for their love and presence in my life.

I thank the remarkable teachers who have helped me on my course: Miss Bortone, McKinley Elementary School, and Dr. Goldstein, Central High School, both of Newark, New

Jersey.

Thank you to the host of friends and colleagues where I have run my figurative marathons in New Jersey, New York, Michigan, Illinois, California, Minnesota and Georgia. And thanks to the thousands of runners who have shared 18 marathons in 11 years. I have plenty of company in wanting to do my personal best.

Thank you to the wonderful students, administrators, faculty, staff and volunteers of Morris Brown College, Chicago State University, University of Minnesota, City University of New York, Claremont Graduate School and Northwestern University who have actively participated in raising our collective consciousness of how to help all individuals succeed, regardless of their ages, races, ethnic and linguistic backgrounds and levels of preparedness. The proceeds from this book will go toward a scholarship fund in my mother's name at Morris Brown College.

Thanks to Vince Tirola when I reached a block—a small wall—in getting on with this manuscript. And a final thank you to James Willis for his love and support.

Dolores E. Cross

Breaking Through the Wall

O Gracious and Eternal God ...

In the midst of life and deeds, it is easy to have endurance and strength and determination, but Thy Word, O Lord, teaches us that this is not enough to bring good to the world—to bring happiness and the worthier success. For this, we must endure to the end—learn to finish things—to bring them to accomplishment and full fruition. We must not be content with plans, ambitions and resolves; with part of a message or part of an education, but be set and determined to fulfill the promise and complete the task and secure the full training. Such men and women alone does God save by lifting them above and raising them to higher worlds and wider prospects. Give us then, O God, strength to resist today the temptation of shirking, and the grit to endure to the end. Amen.

—Dr. William Edward B. Du Bois,
writing in Fountain Hall at Morris Brown College,
one of the highest points in Atlanta

MILE I

Two years after I celebrate my 50th birthday, I run multiple marathons in one year: Grandma's in Duluth, Twin Cities in Minneapolis-St. Paul and the New York City Marathon.

By the time I am running along the streets of New York, my body knows what to do. Feet turn over on their own, knowing they have gone the distance before. By mile 20, my legs feel heavy, and I can feel a tightening in my quadriceps. I am pushing, maintaining a rhythm as I pump my arms and move my feet.

Ahead, walking slowly, is a young black woman, looking dejected, head down. I know without asking that she has hit the wall and wants to get through it. I move to her side, running in place. I learn that this is her first marathon. She has traveled to New York City from California. She expects some friends to be waiting for her at the finish but she doubts if she can make it. Her eyes widen as I tell her my age group and that I've run two marathons already this year.

I've been where she is now and I know she can get through it. We slow down and speed up in intervals, and I continue talking to distract her. "Visualize the finish," I say, running, jogging, running, all the while, for myself as well as for her. "See the banner in your mind. Hear the noise. Greet your friends." She begins to relax and smile when I suggest she imagine that she's a runaway slave, tired, hunted, having to cover as much ground as possible before daylight. "The bark of the dogs has grown faint," she says. I know then that she can do it. I move ahead to the next water stop, confident that she can go it alone.

As I run on, fatigue begins to creep across my body. Suddenly the pain of my back-to-back marathons finds me again. I keep moving, moving, not hearing anything distinguishable, moving, moving. At mile 25.2 I lapse into what seems like delirium, running, running, moving, moving, through the finish line and down the chute, not stopping to tear off my numbered tag.

I feel someone running beside me, touching my arm. "Hey lady,

good job, but the race is over," he exclaims. As I slow to a stop,
breathing hard, I turn to him, just able to say, "No, the race is not
over." I feel suddenly clear, right, appropriately profound in
announcing that only I can declare that the race is over.

The race, the marathon, is a renewal of a belief in one's self and
the ultimate expression of confidence that you have created the foun-
dation that enables you to go the distance. For me, the marathon
began long before the starting gun went off. Just as my training has
readied me physically for the challenge of running 26.2 miles, the
lessons I have learned from the moment of my birth have prepared me
to push forward again and again. I have learned to listen to the
lessons of my life and to go the distance.

I emerged from my mother's womb with a smile on my face.
On a warm summer day in Newark, New Jersey, a few years
before America entered the Second World War, I became the
second of two daughters born to Ozie and Charlie Tucker.
"Dolores, you were born smiling," my mother told me.
"Nurses from all over the hospital came to see you, the little
baby girl with a smile."

The one who wasn't smiling was my father, who had lost
a wager that I would be a boy. He had been so confident about
having a son that he and Ma had not even considered girls'
names. My Aunt Lottie, my mother's younger sister, responded to the urgency of the situation by proposing the name
Dolores after the 1930s star Dolores Del Rio. My middle name,
Evelyn, was suggested by my father's cousin, Henry, in honor
of his girlfriend at the time. So I became Dolores Evelyn Tucker.

Dad and my sister Jean, all of 11 months older than I,
brought me and Ma home from the hospital to our apartment
in a wood-frame, three-flat in Newark.

Charlie Tucker was born in New Rochelle, New York, to
Mary Winston and the Rev. Thomas Timothy Tucker, both of
whom were from Virginia. In his youth, Charlie was the free
spirit among his seven brothers and one sister and the one
most likely to clash with his serious father, a Baptist minister.

He was denied dinner for a week once when he chided his father about a long blessing before a meal. "Pa, you're worrying God to death," he said. He took further risks by skipping school, dancing and gambling on Sundays. At one point, the Rev. Tucker threw him out of the house for truancy and sent him to live at his aunt's home in New Rochelle.

Charlie, a stutterer, dropped out of high school before graduation and took up the trade of dry cleaning. While he was close enough to his brothers and wished them well in their business ventures, he always said he was having more fun than they were. He had a charm about him that his mother and his friends could not resist. Charlie's storytelling included more embellishments than truth. When he said, "Aaah, because ..." you knew not to trust what came next. He loved joining Cousin Henry in excursions to Harlem. As he got ready to go out, he spent time in front of the mirror describing to himself how fine he looked. "Sure look debonair. Dressed like the best," he said as he turned to get the full view. To me, he always looked like the screen star, Keenan Wynn, in brown face, with his receding hairline, mustache and the slight gap in his teeth.

My mother, Ozie, worked in the tobacco fields as a young girl while her father Haywood Johnson tried his hand at farming and contract jobs in stone masonry, building inside water wells and chimneys. Haywood's father was a Cherokee who had been displaced by the government from lands in Oklahoma. He found his way to North Carolina, where he found refuge with a family of slaves.

Haywood Johnson first married Ozie's mother's older sister. When she died, he married Ozie's mother Melissa, who was 45 years younger than he and younger than two of her stepchildren. When Haywood died, Melissa was 34 and had 17 children from two marriages to look after. She sent Ozie at age 14 to live with her sister Lucy in Raleigh, North Carolina, where she was to learn to do something useful. "When she came to us, she could barely do a good job of washing dishes," Lucy said. Ozie learned how to sew as she began school at a government-funded high school for Negroes. Later, she was sent to live with another sister in Chase City, Virginia, where she completed her high school education at a church-supported Presbyterian school. When she finished her schooling, she moved to Newark to work as a seamstress helper and attend night school.

No one would ever have picked my parents out of a crowd as a couple although they had certain similarities in their backgrounds. They shared birth order—second youngest in their large families—and birth sign, Aquarius. My mother's birthday was February 11 and my father's, February 12. Their siblings described them in the same way: odd, offbeat and spirited. But they never looked like they belonged to each other or anyone else, for that matter.

My parents met at a YMCA dance in Newark, where Charlie's family had been an important part of the community for many years. Ozie's family had moved there from North Carolina. She was attracted to his smooth talking. He was taken in by what he called her exotic looks, her upswept hair adorned with flowers and her practiced mysterious look. "It sure wasn't her cooking," he later told anyone who would listen. "Ozie's idea of cooking is lighting a fire under food."

Ozie and Charlie married at a time when Negroes sat at the back of the bus, drank from water fountains marked "Colored Only," attended segregated schools and held mostly menial jobs. In the 1930s, when many black families split themselves into two to find work in different locations, Ozie and Charlie shared a sense that raising good children would have its own reward and provide a sense of accomplishment. They believed this achievement would make things better for all Negroes. In their minds, the worst was over. My parents believed deeply that the contributions Negroes were making during World War II—as they adhered to the constraints of food rationing, bought U.S. War Bonds and responded to calls to serve in the military and work in munitions plants—would lead to the obliteration of discrimination. There was good reason, in their minds, that I was born smiling.

MILE 2

When you run, your past is with you.

"You won't be late for school, if you run fast, run hard. You have the Johnson women's legs. Strong and pretty, they got that way because we worked in the fields, helping Grandma on the farm. Your legs get strong running on the grass. You have to lift your legs when you run on the grass. You can't shuffle. That's why your Ma has strong legs, and you will, too."

My strong legs carry me on, and sometimes I sing:

"Don't you feel my legs or you might get high, and if you get too high, you'll touch my thigh, and if you touch my thigh, you're much too high ... ."

"Why do you teach that girl those songs, Henry?" my mother asked. I was three and singing and dancing as Cousin Henry had taught me. "Look, Ozie," Henry would say, "She doesn't stutter when she sings." Henry Winston was Grandma Tucker's nephew, and like Dad, he had been born in New Rochelle. To hear Ma tell it, he also had been spoiled just like my father. Cousin Henry could be counted on to bring the jokes and songs he'd learned in the jazz clubs of Harlem. He was my companion one Sunday, when my parents dressed Jean and took her off to church. Jean's white dress looked pretty against her light skin as I watched them all go out to the car. "They don't like my little brown monkey, but I do," Cousin Henry said, pouting first and then spinning me around till we were both dizzy with laughter. Just the day before, my mother had been on him for calling me "monkey." When he said he would stop, I cried. "Does it mean you don't love me anymore when you don't call me 'monkey?'" Cousin Henry and Ma both broke out laughing.

Cousin Henry would be with us often for days and weeks at a time. Most often he'd be there to get my father out of the house to play what Ma regarded as that "hateful game of cards" or to offer an explanation of Dad's whereabouts, such as "visiting the sick in the family." Loud, angry voices would melt to music, singing and dancing when Cousin Henry backed up Dad's stories to Ma.

My sister Jean and I would peek through the middle room of our flat to see Ma and Dad gliding happily across the floor and Cousin Henry smiling, because once again, he had gotten Ma to back down from her threats to put both of them out on the street.

The "application" seemed at the time to be all that mattered to Ma. In time, Jean and I realized that the application— which somehow always needed to be checked on—was our request to move into the new housing projects in Newark. There would be more room, so Ma and Dad wouldn't have to sleep in the living room. And we would have hot and cold running water, a new refrigerator and a gas stove.

They agreed on the importance of focusing on having a better life and something to show for their efforts. The opportunity to move to the projects would be a step up. They also made very clear that Jean and I were not to tear down Negroes in our house. And as sisters, Jean and I were to stick together, no matter what. "That's family," Ma or Dad would say.

Cousin Henry had been there to take care of us while my parents went to the hospital to have our baby brother. Jean and I were waiting for our new "little protector." I wondered how big he would be. When they came home from the hospital tired and sad and alone, I knew the baby wasn't coming anymore and that we weren't supposed to talk about it.

Ma and Pa's arguments seemed more frequent, and even Cousin Henry couldn't quell the biggest argument I can remember, one that led to lamps flying and my mother crying and screaming. Ma was still wearing her mourning clothes for the baby. After that fight, Dad and Cousin Henry were away more at my grandparents' house or as Ma said, "out on the town." At times, Dad explained his absence by dropping a pail of freshly caught fish on the floor of the kitchen. We squealed as Cousin Henry raised up a fish and fanned it toward us. Ma sighed and held back a smile. "You'd better hurry up and fry those fish," she said.

When our housing application was accepted, we were to move from our apartment on Fairview Avenue to the segregated public housing project at 200 Orange Street known as Baxter Terrace. Our excitement gave way to new emotions as Ma told us, "Your father isn't coming. He won't be living with us anymore." She had already turned her back when she said, "I don't want to see any crying. Just be glad he took care of the application for the projects."

As I walked down the walk of our apartment for the last time, I looked back at what had been our window on the second floor. I expected Dad or Cousin Henry to appear. No one beckoned us back. We left.

Our new home looked like a mountain of red brick, very different from our three-flat. We stood in the middle of the courtyard as my mother pointed to the utmost third-floor apartment, which was ours. My eyes fastened on a black iron rail protected by glass on the landing separating the second and third floors. I was reminded of the jails my father had pointed out on rides through town and I held my mother's hand tight. Ma, beaming, went on about the magnificence of our new home, our "sugar hill," our new status and the new things we'd find inside. We would feel like royalty. I walked tall like Ma, but I didn't let go of her hand until I was inside the apartment and felt free to run in the hugeness of our four new rooms.

Each day in our new apartment in the housing project took me further from the memories of laughter, singing and dancing on Fairview Avenue. My father moved to Harlem with Cousin Henry and then joined the Merchant Marines. "He'll do anything to avoid child support," Ma said.

At night I looked out of the window in the bedroom that

Jean and I shared. I saw the dome of a faraway building and announced with the authority of a four-year-old, "That's where the princess of my stories lives." To me, it was a magic palace, and the princess was my friend. I knew in my heart that I was right even after my mother told me that my magic palace was the Newark Telephone building on Broad Street.

MILE 3

My body responds to the exhilaration of other runners. The gun sounds, and I know to move slowly, focusing on form and avoiding a surge that will leave me depleted and unable to run a strong race. I find a simple cadence to help me breathe smoothly and settle in to a good pace. The rhythm I find gives me confidence and makes me feel strong. "Relax, release, relate. Relax, release, relate. Relax, release, relate," I say as I glide.

Out of school, through the Italian neighborhood with its smell of garlic and its tailors and shoemakers, across the bridge and over to Orange Street, crowded with cars that honked their turn signals. Past the people on their front stoops, through the courtyard, up the two flights of steps, and to our door.

That's how I returned home each day from kindergarten, always beating my sister Jean to the door. I used the key I wore on a long string around my neck to open the door to the apartment, where we were supposed to wait until my mother came home from work at the munitions war plant.

Jean and I knew that if we failed to do our house chores or got caught outside or with friends inside, that angry voice we'd heard directed at our father would lash out at us—along with the cord from the iron against our legs. What's more, folks had been asked to leave if the manager's surprise inspections found their apartments unkempt or the hallways dirty. Despite the consequences, Jean and I always struggled over who would do what before my mother returned home for two hours and had to go out again to evening classes at the YMCA. Jean would set me in a panic by focusing on one corner of the room for what seemed like forever. My mother would never ask who did what but would be on both of us if we didn't get it right. The beds had to be made, the floors cleaned, the bathroom and kitchen shined, and dinner started. Starting dinner meant opening and heating the contents of a few cans.

Sometimes we had time for playing the card game, War, or doing what Jean called interpretive dances. We followed whatever was on the radio: "When a Girl Marries," "Portia Faces Life" and "The Shadow." From our living room window, we'd watch other children play outside. We'd also stare across the courtyard trying to catch sight of Marian and Virginia, two bullying sisters who often taunted us. My mother called them "wild," and threatened that if we weren't "careful," we'd end up like them. She never elaborated, so we searched for physical signs. Our friends said it had to do with "the nasty," and we pretended we knew what they were talking about.

The neighbors below always thumped on the ceiling as we ran through our apartment playing tag or hide-and-seek. One day, Mrs. Veasey below us met my mother in the hall after Ma had just finished her usual nine hours at the munitions plant. She proceeded to give her a lesson on how to rear children. At 6 and 5, Jean and I could have told Mrs. Veasey that the end of the day was the wrong time to cross Ma. They had words and pushed and shoved each other. After the incident, Mrs. Veasey's daughters Rose and Esther terrorized us, pretending we were war enemies to be stabbed with sticks they called bayonets.

There were two boys on the second floor who seemed much nicer than any of the girls we had met. When Ma warned us about the company of boys, it was hard to comprehend because they were such easy-going sorts.

My mother encouraged Jean and me to be close. She dressed us alike and made us have joint birthday celebrations. She even wanted us to avoid other children. "You two have each other to entertain," she said. "You don't need to be hanging around outside."

We didn't have a lot of friends. With Ma's attitude at home, we were sure to go our separate ways outside. We never went to and from school together. Jean was embarrassed by my stuttering, and I didn't want to be identified with her fooling around in school.

Yet I worried about her when the air raid siren sounded to signal a drill. We had to scurry for cover amidst reminders that the drill could be a real attack. Pearl Harbor could happen again, everyone said. And then Jean and I would forever be separated in the rubble of Newark. We had to follow the wartime rules.

But sometimes we conspired to thwart my mother's rules. Down Orange Street I would bound, mindful of my mission and allotted time. I'd run past the neighborhood stores and wood-frame houses south of the projects, past a small factory and through the smell of the popcorn at the Treat movie theatre. Finally, I made a right turn at Broad Street. First, I went to the Newark Public Library, feeling the bumps of the books in the stacks and scanning their titles as I hurried through, glancing at the clock. Then, I went to the Newark Museum on the next block, where I could walk in the quiet and touch even more things. They told me to touch, to push buttons at the exhibits. I observed faces moving and things being transformed: rocks changing colors, engines leaping as pistons moved. I gawked at my favorite, the shining knight's armor near the door. I wanted to tell Ma about it, but of course I couldn't. And I hurried home to make it there before she arrived at six o'clock.

Ma said she was doing the best she could for us. "I moved you girls to Baxter Terrace. I keep us going all on my own," she said. But we didn't know what to make of her painting each wall a different color or buying books that we couldn't read. She bought a piano, although she could not afford lessons for us, and she had us featured at the piano in the social pages of the *Afro-American News* as if we were playing. All I learned was the piano scale, "Mary Had a Little Lamb" and one verse of "Auld Lang Syne," from the beginners piano book she purchased.

Ma encouraged us to show off our strengths. We could be asked at any family social gathering to recite a poem, sing or share what we were doing in school. Most often we'd be asked to spell a simple word or multiply two numbers. Even if I stuttered, I knew I would be encouraged or applauded and that others would be chastised if they laughed as my lips shook or my face twisted. I was meant to move ahead and get through it.

My Grandmother Tucker told me not to let obstacles get in the way of what was inside. "It's in you, child," she said as she waited for me to speak. " It's yours. Hold on. Let it come out." In my mind, I heard both my stutter and the words that were in me. And with her coaxing, I could speak. I could get through it.

Times like those unfortunately couldn't compensate for when classmates laughed or mimicked my halting, pained voice. One day I had to visit my sister's class to tell her teacher she would not be in school that day. I stood before the teacher and struggled and sputtered to get out "Miss" and when it wouldn't come forth, I called out "Hey" to her. "Hay is for horses," she said to guffaws from the class. Shamed, I stood there for a moment and ran out the door, the laughter still strong at my back.

MILE 4

Gotta get past this. Some pain is breaking through. No, it's too early to tighten. Gotta get through this bad spell, black spell. I have so much farther to go. It's scary—this feeling of self doubt and sudden pointed pain. Stay focused, dig down. On the verge of hysteria. Breathe deep. Persist. Get through it. Keep moving.

It began with the ringing of the doorbell one night while my mother worked the night shift at the plant. Jean and I went to the door and asked who was there. A man's voice responded, "Mr. Rice, a friend of your mother's."

I am not sure what else he said or why we opened the door to let him in. Once inside, he went into my mother's room and called us to the bed where he had stretched out. Both of us went to him obediently. He began touching me. I cried, but he continued groping, hurting me, moving to my sister and then back to me. He was steadfast in moving my hand to him. I sent my mind to other places as he felt my body, filling me with a lingering, dark fright.

After a time, when he let me, I slid away. Jean was already gone. I got into my own bed, crying and afraid of the man in our apartment and seized with the fear of what my mother would do if she knew I had let someone in the house. I was scared. I had disobeyed. She might punish me even more.

The man left before morning came. Jean and I did not speak to each other of that night, nor did we tell my mother.

There had been talk and pictures in the newspaper about a little girl who had been murdered and put in the incinerator. Her mother was found lying dead in a blood-filled bathtub. The little girl, Sadie, was seven and had lived not too far from me in the projects. I wondered if Sadie had opened the door to a stranger. Had she disobeyed her mother, too, and let in someone who hurt her? Ma and all her friends had speculated about who the murderer might be. I strained to hear from a seat I had taken outside the kitchen door while the conversation moved from Sadie to all the things that had happened to them or to a friend when they were growing up. Maimings, babies falling, houses burning, rapes, broken limbs, busted lips and minds lost. "Stuff like this happens all the time," my mother said. "We've got to keep it together. I have to leave my girls alone with only my prayers."

In the nights that followed, I couldn't fall asleep until the early hours of the morning. I would feel my mother tugging at me to hurry or I'd be late to school. I heard her displeasure as she found I had wet my bed. My bed-wetting became a frequent occurrence. I'd get up early to rinse the yellow ring, cover the spot with a towel or, if there was time, put the sheet on the radiator to dry. I couldn't tell her I was too frightened to leave my bed and go to the bathroom.

My stuttering became more pronounced and I was told again and again, "Take your time" and "Slow down."

We had been in the projects for three years before that night with the stranger. A fleeting collage of events filled my head. I had a sense of a string of moving pictures of our move, our new furniture, our new friends, the starting of school, the chores we had, Ma's work and school. I searched through these images to find one to lull me to sleep. Yet on most nights, I heard the doorbell again in my dreams, saw the stranger and experienced the whole night again in slow motion. Morning was a faraway promise. I had to get through the night.

MILE 5

As I begin a race I select a runner with a pace a notch above mine and focus on his or her running shoes, maintaining a distance, yet keeping the runner in sight. If the lead runner slows, I'll pick up my pace and pass and seek a faster pair of running shoes to follow.

I'm aware of other people around me, yet I keep the lead runner in sight as if I'm being pulled. There are others behind me, and I fancy I'm the lead runner for someone else. I try to stay focused, looking ahead. I pump my legs and arms. I do not look back.

My mother felt it was important to keep up the ties to the Tuckers, so she sent us by bus early Saturday or late Friday to stay with them through the evening service on Sunday. My grandmother kept us busy so that our grandfather, the Rev. Tucker, was almost unaware of our treks to their home on Miller Street. Without even knowing the stories about my father's dealings with the Rev. Tucker, whom we called "Pa," we found him humorless and formal. He spent most of his time reading the *Bible* or books about his mission in Haiti. He was born three years after the end of the Civil War on a plantation in Virginia. Orphaned at an early age, he dedicated himself at barely age 20 to the ministry. At 23, he was a pastor of the North Clinton Baptist Church in East Orange and went on to found other churches in Passaic, Summit, Montclair, Rutherford and finally Union Baptist Church in Newark in 1907. In his lifetime of service, he chaired the Board of the Newark Community Hospital and served as dean of ministers in the Baptist Ministry. He earned a doctorate in divinity from the Afro-American School of Correspondence in Washington, D.C. He commanded the respect of his congregation.

Jean and I shared a bed with my grandmother in a small room across the hall from the large library and bedroom occupied by my grandfather. We would travel with her to

Bamberger's store on Saturday, pushing the small of her broad back as she climbed the hill to the bus stop. My grandmother took great pleasure in waking us up to the smell of hot rolls and the promise of a small pan of our own, to be taken with jam and tea at the dining room table before Pa came down for breakfast. On Sundays, we had the joyful duty of delivering rolls that she sold to her neighbors for 5 cents to 20 cents a pan. She would grumble to us about the $10 a week she received from my grandfather for meals and running the house. She made do by bargaining with vendors from horse-drawn wagons laden with vegetables, fruits or blocks of ice for the ice box. She also traded with the junkman, an apple pie for a small appliance. Despite her efforts, Pa often sent his food back to be cooked again or in some different way. Except for the meals that he ate with his sons, he ate alone at the large dining room table and seemed not to notice us as we served him.

When Jean and I were ages 8 and 7, Grandmother Tucker decided we should be baptized. My mother made special dresses for us, and we spent a large portion of Saturday getting our hair pressed and curled. We did not look forward to losing all the luster in our hair—and the compliments—after our dip in the water of the baptismal pool. Nervous and excited, I was led to the edge of the pool, which was in a recessed area in the floor under the pulpit. My grandfather helped me down into the pool and then held my body as he dunked me into the water. I realized that I had never felt his arms around me. He held me securely as he supported my neck and back. I felt safe.

Mrs. Dasher, a church elder, took it upon herself to advise Jean and me about what was expected of us as the pastor's grandchildren. She seemed to be an extension of my grandfather with her no-nonsense approach. We were to follow her instructions and pace as junior ushers and be on time for every Sunday school class, church service, afternoon function, Baptist Young Peoples Union meeting and evening service. She impressed upon us what baptism meant in terms of making a contribution to the congregation, but she impressed upon us even more what being a Tucker meant. The Tucker brothers, with the notable exception of my father, were leaders in the community, businessmen who could be counted on to help others. "Those boys could go to any of those big churches," Mrs. Dasher said, "but they are here every Sunday."

My uncles were just as disciplined in taking time for dinners with Grandfather Tucker as they were in going to church. Pa acted very different with his sons than he did with my grandmother and his fair-skinned, blue-eyed daughter, my Aunt Carolyn, who was just as shrewd in business as her brothers and bristled when taken for white. We would hear my uncles laughing with their father as they discussed their experiences as Pullman porters and the virtues of an investment opportunity in Liberia. They'd talk about getting the Negroes out to vote and the importance of education if things were to get better. They also discussed the risks they'd be taking to open their own insurance agency in a house on Orchard Street. They were proud as well of having volunteered and served in the armed forces.

Jean and I reminded them of their youngest brother Charlie. Their sentences would begin, "Charlie's got a good heart, but—." They referred to us as Charlie's kids, not as their nieces.

Sometimes my father managed to be at our grandparents' house when we visited on weekends. One Saturday he announced he was taking us to Harlem. We were happy to be with him, standing on the train platform in Newark, just waiting for the train. Our delight, however, was interrupted by a loud, drunk white sailor.

"Get out of my way! Move your black nigger ass out of my way," he said, and shoved my father. My father pushed us gently behind him and went at that man with a fury that set us to tears. A red cap saw the fight and ran over to pull my father back. "Brother, you don't want to hit him. You got those girls over there," he said. The red cap continued to beg my father to stop as the train approached. My father dropped the stunned sailor and grabbed us and we all jumped on the train.

He was quiet for the whole trip. When we arrived at the

restaurant he wanted to take us to, nothing about the meal seemed to please him. It was when I began to cry that he changed back to the person I knew, and he began making jokes about how Grandma could show the cooks a thing or two about food.

And then he went on as he always did, each story getting more lavish in the retelling. We heard about his achievement in competition among dry cleaners where he pressed pants in record time, although he lamented that he came in second to an Italian. He laughed when we told him about his brothers giving us money for getting to church on time on Sundays, only to take it away if we did not say thank you.

My mother wanted to make sure we knew about our heritage on both sides of the family, so she began sending us by bus to her mother's house. Grandma Johnson was glad to see us, but her dark house was always filled with other grandchildren, and she had a lot less variety in the food that she served. Most often we'd have molasses, bread baked on her wood stove and thick slices of bacon. She always expected us to do all the talking.

Ma was insistent that we know how she grew up so she sent us away for two summers to live with our cousins on a tobacco farm outside Raleigh, North Carolina. My Aunt Lucy came for us by train. We'd spend a week with her and Uncle Noah, and then they'd drive us to the tobacco farm to help out.

My cousins lived in a two-room wooden shack. There were eight of us children to sleep on pallets in a room that was also a kitchen. In the mornings, we'd be awakened and given a breakfast of biscuits, syrup and buttermilk. I detested buttermilk. We boarded troughs pulled by mules to get to the tobacco fields, where our job was to kill the worms. My cousins rolled with laughter as I pushed the fat worms off the leaves and attempted to squash them with my feet. They reached over and snapped them with their fingers, making me scream in disgust.

One day, I fell off the mule trough and hit my head, slicing my ear. My cousin pressed my bleeding ear hard, filling the gash with charcoal from the stove. While I rested and she pressed, she told me stories about my mother. My mother had hidden under her bed to avoid having to go on the trough to the tobacco fields.

At night I told the stories I knew from school and from my reading until the room was quiet or I fell asleep in the middle of a story. Jean and I had a special place of honor with them as we played school with them. The work during my summer weeks with them was so much fun, I wondered to myself, "How could Ma miss such fun?"

We went from our work in the fields back to Raleigh to spend time with Aunt Lucy and Uncle Noah. Uncle Noah made sure I understood the "Colored Only" signs on the restrooms, water fountains and sections in the movies and other public places. For ten cents, we could enter the balcony, see white people sitting below us in the orchestra section and watch the show.

My uncle wanted to spoil us with treats, and he worried because he knew we had yet to learn all the rules of the South. When I reached for an ice pop in a self-serve refrigerator in a neighborhood store, he didn't have time to prepare me for the proprietor's anger. "Nigger, get your hand out of there," the man yelled. Uncle Noah secured my hand and led me out of the store as tears swelled in my eyes. His hand was warm, and his face had broken out in a sweat. But his face was expressionless and his voice audible only to me. "Keep walking and don't look back," he said.

MILE 6

Where do my feelings come from? I can't do this, can't run this far. It is like going through endless transition in childbirth, with no joyous uncontrollable push to get you to the next level. Body, don't rebel. Breathe deep, breathe deep. Feel the ground under your feet. Get past what you don't want to do. Do it, relax and don't be held back.

My mother struggled to get child support from my father. He'd come by to see us but she wouldn't let him in. One summer night, he stood below our window in the courtyard, calling "Ozie!" and demanding to see his children. She responded by throwing an ashtray out the window at him. At that point, she told us to call the police if he attempted to see us again because she was reporting him for failure to pay child support.

My father waited till my mother was in the hospital for minor surgery before he tried to see us again. We were staying at the home of my mother's friend, whom we called Aunt Fifi. We saw Dad out Aunt Fifi's second-floor window. While he rang the bell, I called the police and said, "My father is here and my mother says I am to call you to report him." He rang and rang until the police came. I looked out the window as they led him away. His face was pained as he looked up to me. I wanted to run out to him. I'd done what my mother wanted, but I felt awful. My father had to spend the night in jail before being released to his brother Roger, who blamed me for the trouble.

Aunt Fifi took me to visit my mother, who was very happy and proud of me. I wanted to forget the whole thing, but my mother insisted I tell the story again and again of how "Charlie had been taken off by the cops." Her friends thought it was hilarious. "You're just like your mother," said one friend who was laughing so hard she could barely speak. I wanted to tell them all it wasn't true. I loved my father. My mother did not. I was not like her. I would go to the mirror and deny any resemblance. I'd liken my mother to the wicked witch of my stories. She ruled and punished us. I thought often of Cinderella and her happy ending. A prince would come, or perhaps my father would return.

Would a prince like me? I measured beauty with the images I saw in magazines, newspapers and the movies. These were pictures, still and moving, of white women. They were the movie stars, beauty and prom queens with long, straight hair and often big Betty Grable bangs or hair luxuriously swept to one side, over the eye, like Veronica Lake. Or there was Shirley Temple, with pink cheeks and a burst of curls. Oh, to have lighter skin and straight, long hair! I was willing to sit perfectly still in the beauty shop chair as the hairdresser pulled the hot comb through my thick hair till my eyes smarted. Once, in my quest for straight hair, she burned me by accident on my ears and the nape of my neck. Nevertheless, the hairdresser gave me a more acceptable self.

My mother didn't take us to the beauty salon often enough for me to feel acceptable all the time. I blamed my mother's dressing us in her homemade ill-fitting dresses when a friend, Judy, excluded me from her birthday celebration. Judy and her family had moved out of the projects to East Orange. When she still lived here, I called her every morning and we walked to school together, but she invited others and not me to her party. My mother didn't make me feel better. "She never came by for you," she said. "They think they're better than us."

I wanted to say something, but I dared not speak back to Ma, when she would go on about how she had "to work so hard and still go to school because your father isn't providing child support." She was driving him and my friends away. I felt Jean and I were raising ourselves. Yet I could not say this to her.

The occasional unpredictable fun times with my father meant more to me than my mother's daily presence and the predictable events of going to the grocery store, music store or market. She never had any stories like my father's, but instead instructed us on how to sit up straight and walk tall. We were to imitate her glide, heads up like queens. She told us never to respond if men called out to us.

At the same time, Ma pressed us to understand the insult Marian Anderson had endured in being barred by the Daughters of the American Revolution from singing at Constitution Hall in Washington, D.C., and what it meant when she had an opportunity to sing at the Lincoln Memorial. We heard her records, saw her pictures and felt my mother's involvement in what Marian Anderson experienced as if it were Ma's personal pain.

One day Ma came home from work and sat with her face in her hands, crying. "He was a great man. He was good for Negroes. We got a chance to work and more respect. And now he's dead." She sobbed and my sister, Jean, began to cry as well. Jean was always able to give adults the smiles and frowns they wanted, and this was a fine display of her talent. Jean peeked between her fingers and winked at me, shrugging to let me know she didn't know any more than I did what had happened, but felt she should help by crying, too. Between her outbursts, Ma said, "President Roosevelt died." Jean and I could only feel relief.

My mother's days were filled with working clerical jobs. She attended classes at night. During breaks at home, we'd see her face relax and hear her sigh pleasantly when we'd show off for her. I'd sweep my hair up like Lena Horne and attempt a sultry singing of "Stormy Weather." And Jean would jump and move expressively, providing her rendition of Katherine Dunham. We'd bang on the piano and request that Ma salute us with singing her favorite, "Desert Song."

Each day Ma went off to work and left instructions for us to "behave." One day, she returned home to find my hand bleeding where Jean had stabbed me with the scissors, the result of another argument over chores. I went for high drama as my mother walked in and declared that Jean had tried to stab me to death. Jean had pleaded with me not to tell. My mother's face said more than words: she felt betrayed. My mother whipped us both.

The incident persuaded my mother that we needed a change. She did a lot of research on camps before she arranged to send us away to Camp Forest Lake in New Hampshire for a few weeks in the summer. We were 12 and 13. For the first time in our lives, we spent time away from her with people who were not family members. Jean and I were in different groups, which meant I didn't get drawn into the fights Jean somehow managed to get in the middle of.

The bus ride to New Hampshire was a dream come true as I watched the homes and towns give way to forests. My favorite poem was Joyce Kilmer's "Trees," which I could recite almost without a stammer. I felt a special connection to trees, as if they knew they were more important to me than they were to other people. At camp, I felt safe and happy amid the leaves. I spent days floating in a rowboat, moving only to get different views of the trees around the lake. I took to painting trees in art classes.

A few days before the end of my time in tree heaven, I was asked to row across the lake with another camper. When the subject of swimming came up, the counselor learned I didn't know how to swim. She was dismayed at everyone's having assumed I could swim, given how I had taken to rowing every day. In the remaining two days of camp, the counselors tried mightily, but they didn't succeed in teaching me to swim.

MILE 7

The start of every race is an echo of my first race.

The announcer blares, "Runners get set!" The gun sounds. My body tenses and acknowledges I'm in it. My eyes dart to the lead relay runner. Her head is back, legs and arms pumping. Her intensity is electrifying. She's ahead, passing the baton. I'm watching, keeping legs and baton in sight. A set of legs is hurtling toward me and I reach for the baton. I'm off in a flash, looking ahead, and safely, quickly, pressing the baton in my teammate's hand. We're still ahead... depending on the anchor.

Yes! Yes! We've done it! My sixth-grade class has come in first place in Newark's All-City Track Meet. I've run my first race well.

It was sunny and beautiful outside. I was 13 and in class. Miss Bortone asked what the term was for warm late autumn days like the one we were experiencing. Hands shot up around the classroom, but she looked at me for the answer. I had written a story about Indian summer, and she knew I could answer the question. She knew, too, that I would be reluctant to answer because I would be mocked for my stuttering. I imagined my face contorting and the words sticking like a phonograph needle on a scratched record if I tried to speak. I said nothing. Miss Bortone looked away and gave the class the answer.

At the end of the day she called me to her desk and commented about how much she liked my stories. She had decided that I should write the eighth-grade graduation play. I was overjoyed! I beamed. I said, "Thank you," and bolted from the room to go home to tell my mother. I ran past the Italian shops, past the Catholic church, to the bridge over the railroad yard, through the courtyard to our apartment.

I expected to find my mother at home, quiet, sad and bent over her sewing machine. She had committed herself to finish-

ing winter coats for my sister and me. I wanted to distract her
with my good news. She had stopped working weeks and
weeks ago—just all of a sudden. At first we'd hear her talk
about what happened. We knew how proud she was to have
been the first black woman in the state of New Jersey to pass a
civil service exam to be a telephone operator. She was assigned
to a position in Hoboken. She had felt her supervisors had
purposely sent her into hostile redneck territory. Her co-work-
ers would rearrange her desk, ignore her and give her wrong
numbers. One day someone left a dead mouse in her desk
drawer. Every day she had to report a new difficulty to her
supervisors. And then she stopped working and started
sewing alone at home. She went out only to buy fabric for a
blue coat for me and a brown one for my sister.

I ran up the steps to give her the good news. There was a
big, shiny new lock on our apartment door. I tried my key,
again and again. I rang, and there was no answer. The anger
rose in my throat. The reality of the new lock washed over me.
The manager had acted on his threat to seize our apartment if
my mother failed to pay the rent again! I wheeled around and
lit out for the manager's office across the courtyard where I
expected to find my mother. She wasn't there, but the manager's red hair and pink face were within view through the open
door as he sat behind his desk.

My questions were labored but hot. "Why?" "Why now,
when she has been late before?" "She followed the rules."
"We've lived here for almost 10 years." "Christmas is coming."
"What will happen to our things?" I was standing up to him
but he ignored me. I left, feeling empty. I found my mother on
a bench in the courtyard, alone and silent in the shadows of the
warm December day.

The Salvation Army in Newark was in a red brick building on Central Avenue, a few blocks from Broad Street. We settled there that night, listening to the cars thundering by in
sharp contrast to our quiet courtyard. My mother and sister
asked me to tell and re-tell my words to the manager. My voice
rang out across the beaten linoleum floor in the room of cots. I

lowered my voice and told them again and again. Ma and Jean made me feel that somehow we hadn't lost everything behind the shiny lock. After they drifted off, I thought of my mother's blank stares, her nervous gestures, her helplessness. And then I retreated to what had happened in school, my being asked to write the eighth-grade play. "Indian summer, Indian summer" I said to myself in belated answer to Miss Bortone as I too fell asleep.

My mother decided to commit herself to a mental hospital, so there was no hiding anything from the relatives anymore. She was 32 years old. Uncle Sam picked us up from the shelter and took us to live first with my grandparents and then with him and Aunt Jean. Ma didn't get to see my eighth-grade play. We begged to be able to visit my mother, but we were not prepared for the frightened look in her eyes and her hair gone wild when we went to the hospital. She had been given shock treatments. We left and did not return to see her in that place. She remained there for six months and then went to live in a boarding house. Our rituals, our things, were gone. No longer could I imagine myself as royalty living where I could see the castle dome. My mother had seen to that.

MILE 7.8

A running dream of me at 13 comes into my consciousness in the form of questions. Who am I? What do I know about me? Am I afraid of someone reading what is true?

The answers flow. I am Dolores at 13. Full of pain, close to wisdom, yet far from any articulation. I can be me, without wanting to be someone else. I am quite satisfied now with my own sculpture, although my mother would disagree. There was some shaping on her part, but it seems, in her preoccupation, a negative design. I willfully decided to undo that design.

When did the convincing begin that I was someone special? Looking at the carving on my new maple bed, I saw a boat and began to fantasize about other places. For years, I studied the boat, touched it and visualized where it was going. Who were the people on the boat? What would I learn from them? Would they share the magic of having moved from place to place? Are they all going to be "moving to the top?" Are they going to be able to stay there or will they lose direction?

Without my mother knowing, I drifted off to sea, to other places I needed to visit.

Now I run there.

Jean and I continued to live with various members of our family, with Aunt Jean and Uncle Sam or Aunt Carrie and Uncle Harrison having us during the week and our grandparents having us on the weekends. After school we'd have the job of cleaning the Tucker Brothers Insurance Agency. Our spare time on the weekends was spent babysitting for neighbors and my aunt.

A team of two once our mother was gone, Jean and I mastered how to look out for each other. Jean knew how to ingratiate us with others and make each entry into the relatives' homes easier. She'd walk in, spot something to ooh about and effusively compliment whatever struck her fancy. I handled the inevitable school questions, since I always had an "A" paper to share.

We also covered for each other when we learned how to advance small amounts of money to ourselves from the cash sent by clients to my uncles' insurance agency. We planned how we would save our money to pay the back rent and get back together with Ma. But the cents here and there were not enough.

Jean had an appendicitis operation when she was 15, while I spent the summer working full time as a bus girl in a downtown cafeteria. I was 14, and my supervisor remarked that I was a fast learner. Generally, I did fine. But my quickness got me into real trouble when, after an hour of observing an older woman reading, with a quarter of a donut and a half cup of cold coffee before her, I cleared the table. She screeched for me to retrieve everything after it'd been thrown down the chute. She left declaring that she wouldn't be back again. Despite that moment, by the end of the summer I had saved $81.

My second summer of working full time was in Brooklyn. I'd seen a "Help Wanted" sign on a visit to my father's place that spring. I was 15, yet I managed to pass for 18 so I could secure the factory job welding metal forks into plastic handles. I saved everything I earned.

In every relative's home, my sister and I were made to feel that people cared about us. In return, we were to practice service at home, in the church, in our extended family and in the community. We'd hear from our uncles who should be supported politically because of fairness to Negroes and who could be counted on to give us a chance with jobs. Generosity and selflessness was an ideal. Simply earning good grades wasn't enough. "Have you learned how to think?" my uncles would ask. "What will what you have learned mean to the community?"

With each compliment, each vote of confidence, and each response to a job well done came the reminder that I had more to do, that my journey was just beginning. I felt at times that nothing was enough and that I would never get there—wherever "there" was. From my family, I heard "thank you" followed by "what's next?"

I began to appreciate different forms of contribution. While my mother damned my father for lack of child support, he gave in other ways, such as when he snapped us up and off to New York to see the circus. How could all those people fit in that little car in the center of the ring? I asked. With total confidence in me, he urged me to figure it out and howled with delight when I answered, "There must be a door in the floor."

And I even started to appreciate my mother when I realized how she must have felt taking us to the chicken market with only enough money to purchase a bag of chicken feet, which she boiled and had us savor as delicacies.

And then there was the opposite of a contribution, a diminution. I felt that when Mary Lou, a young white friend, avoided me in classes, hallways and play areas after we had spent one summer writing to each other sharing our adventures, drawings and photos. I had thought we were the best of friends. But she had been told not to play with the colored girl. We had written to each other, yet only lived three blocks apart.

MILE 8

We began the race at 7 a.m. on a course along Lake Superior. There were few spectators during the first half. A feeling both relaxed and powerful engulfed me. I felt connected with the trees, water and air with the lifting of my arms and legs. I felt at peace yet fully aware, alive, strong, as my feet drummed along the road. Determination as fierce as the wind can see us through.

By the end of my second summer of work, we were able to add to what my mother had saved to pay the back rent and move to an apartment in another housing project, Seth Boyden.

We had looked forward to being together again, but it proved difficult for all of us. Jean and I had grown more independent in our absence from my mother. We were not used to her telling us what to do anymore. We had lived with different family members and learned to adjust to different temperaments, while still being bound to her. After all that time of doing our best for her yet without her, we were not sure what was next.

In the time away from us, my mother returned to evening school and began taking and passing civil service exams on a routine basis. Yet she wouldn't accept a job, and much of the time she appeared satisfied just to be in the room with us to hear of our days and each new achievement at school.

But sometimes, she raged. She demanded us to see or do something her way, and she railed against the depths of racial discrimination in our country. Discrimination hadn't lessened despite the contributions of Negroes in the war effort, the breakthroughs by Jackie Robinson, the successes of Thurgood Marshall and even what she, Ozie, had sacrificed and done for her daughters.

She accepted welfare payments while protesting the government's issuing of cheese and powdered eggs to a population prone to hypertension. Welfare itself was necessary and appropriate, given racism, she said. She never let up on her cheese protest, despite being alone in her views.

She'd speak to us and expect of us just as if we'd been away for a weekend and not two years. She had not, as my uncles hoped, "mellowed."

My mother's time away from us had been a mystery to us. But we sought to connect this mystery to our own lives by telling Ma the stories of what we'd experienced. At her urging, we'd go back to the beginning and speak of how our grandparents had moved us out of Grandmother Tucker's little room to the middle bedroom on the second floor of their home on Miller Street. Our grandfather would come in sometimes and shine a flashlight on us to check if we were there and sleeping. Cousin Henry joined us at their home when it was discovered he had pneumonia.

Henry's presence made it easier for us. He was always supportive of me, calling me "Bright Eyes." He could point out to my grandfather the benefits of Jean and me helping Grandmother Tucker keep up the coal furnace and empty and clean his slop jar. Cousin Henry also managed what I'd thought was impossible. My grandfather began to soften toward me, as Henry got him to listen to me practice my clarinet for the Central High School marching band. They both found great amusement in referring to me and my playing as Edgar Allan Poe's "Lost Lenore." Pa would join in and slur it to say, "lost manure."

After that, Pa took more note of me to the point of deciding he would call me "Hope." He said, "Granddaughter, I'm going to call you Hope, like the *Bible*'s 'Faith, Hope and Charity.'" The new name, however, gave him the latitude to call me "Hopeless" when, to his thinking, I failed to display common sense. One day, I invited a male friend to visit Miller Street so we could collaborate on a school project. Having a young man in the house was something a young woman in her right mind should not do, to my grandfather's thinking. When the young man came over, my grandfather wasted no time in calling him up to his room and giving him a talking to that sent him running from the house.

This story brought a broad smile to my mother's face. Always worried that Jean and I would get into boy trouble, she was glad my grandfather's strict rules overcame my grandmother's tendency to trust us and give in. She'd felt that Grandmother Tucker had spoiled my father and let him get away with too much and would, if left alone, spoil us as well.

We saw it differently. Grandmother Tucker just treated us special, made us feel special with small gestures. She saw to it that there was a hard roll and an apple for my lunch. She'd make my sandwich exactly as I wanted. We were permitted to play with the neighbors' children, and she was always home when we returned from school.

Our time with her was spent in the kitchen where we learned both from what she said and the strength we would see on her expressive face. On Wednesday nights we'd join her for prayer meeting. We'd be the only children there, basking in the praise of the church sisters when we'd pray and always include a special prayer to ask God to bring us together again with our mother. My grandmother brought a special hush of silence to the church as she'd stand up tall, getting ready to close the meetings with a singing of "Precious Lord." We heard a voice much deeper, richer and louder than we'd ever hear on Miller Street.

We told Ma of how it had been to stay with Aunt Jean and Uncle Sam and how they had managed to get some of our books and kitchenware stored in their apartment to keep the housing authorities from discarding it. Aunt Jean's place was the loveliest home I had ever seen. Her French provincial furniture had fine lines, soft pink and light blue tones in the needlepoint chairs. A delicate table was inlaid with flowers. Aunt Jean had saved and saved from working in the home of whites who treated her as family and paid her well. She did not marry my Uncle Sam until she had acquired her furniture.

We lived in a room that had been hers, sleeping under pink and blue sheets with pillows filled with little feathers.

Aunt Jean required us to wear stockings, gloves and hats to church and always listened to make sure we washed our hands after flushing the toilet. Her voice was soft, delicate and gentle. My uncle worried that she was tiring in trying to help us.

I'd hear them all night. Uncle Sam spoke of the roaches—which he called "permanent residents"—that had been in the things from our apartment. Aunt Jean would speak of how difficult it must be for Jean and me drifting among the relatives, missing our mother and taking public transportation to our old neighborhood. She worried that with all that moving we did not have special friends.

We made sure Ma knew that her sisters also were pleased to see us and fed us well. She was passionate about us learning about and appreciating being part of a family, a family that included the Tuckers, the Johnsons and people in the church and neighborhood who cared about us. In return, we supplied her with every detail to which she added stories from her childhood to help us with connections.

While she wanted to hear our stories, she twisted our reports into evidence that others were trying to take credit for us. She had done the best she could for us, and all by herself, she said. I would see her fist clench and jaws tighten as she spoke of the Tuckers. We were her children, she said.

As she had in Baxter Terrace, Ma felt that the three of us should keep to ourselves for company. But time hadn't stopped for us; we couldn't go back to those lonely days. My mother knew she was no longer our center, our anchor, but she wanted us to feel she was a good mother. She was proud of my working summers to save toward the unpaid rent money, and she wanted to make sure we were proud of her achievement in continuing to go to evening school and being involved in the Negro Women's Business and Professional Club. Being a good mother meant achieving. Achievements were meant to ameliorate what couldn't be changed.

Jean and I took to making friends at school, knowing that we wouldn't be able to invite them to our place. Jean's circle of friends took her back to Baxter Terrace where she was well liked for her ability to put people at ease and make people laugh. We were together in adjusting to the difficulties of being with Ma. We both had to stand up to her when her demands and efforts to cut us off were too painful. It didn't feel good having to block her verbal and physical blows. We realized soon after our reunion with Ma that the way out was getting a job and marrying early.

In her senior year of high school, Jean was fending off suitors. I began to think with dread what it might be like at home without my sister. I was flattered to no end when a suitor came by for Jean when she was out and remarked, "I didn't know she had a good-looking sister like you." This could be my ticket out, I thought.

Finding the right guy was no small task. This meant someone hardworking, or as my mother would say, "upstanding." This also meant someone clean, neat and mannerly. These traits, plus being a good dancer, added up to a "swell guy." And should he have "good" hair, fair skin and a job at the post office, you would have died and gone to Heaven. Courtships tended to be pursued while assessing what your offspring might look like. We grew up observing that the darker you were, the less likely you would be a favorite or have the socially mobile job of an elevator operator or Pullman porter. And we wanted to believe that as the laws changed so would the complexion of the prince and the princess.

In my senior year, I imagined my place in the graduation procession. If they lined us up by height or alphabetically, either way I'd be at the end of the line. I dreamed of leading my class and worked to achieve a class rank to make it so. I was devastated when my typing teacher caused my 3.9 average to plummet with a "C." But my hopes were renewed when Dr. Goldstein, my English teacher, requested that in honor of his retirement the high school graduation speaker would be selected from among the seniors who wrote the best essays. I knew I was in the running. I'd leave school every day and head straight for the library to research and write and rewrite for hours. I wrote from my heart about the impact of Lincoln's

Gettysburg Address in motivating a vision of a different America and encouraging protests in the 1950s. One word led to another word, as I wrote. I felt encouraged by my family. I tried out my thoughts on Uncle Sam and saw him beam. At times I would be reluctant to talk about my essay; I didn't want to lose my way. I knew as I worked that what I was writing was in good form, well paced and spirited like a sermon.

While I was writing the essay, I spent time at my grandparents, most often in my grandfather's room, watching, helping as he changed the dressings on the ulcers on his foot and seeing him grow weaker. He still responded to Henry's attempts to cheer him but was more and more distracted as he worried about his church and the congregation that was his family.

Pa had sadly delegated the leadership of Union Baptist Church to his assistant pastor. The Rev. Paul's foot-stomping, pulpit-slapping, body-swaying and word-singing approach to soul saving contrasted sharply with my grandfather's quiet yet intense lectures. The Rev. Paul declared he was there to "wake 'em up," while Uncle Roger said he was nothing but a "jack leg preacher intent on tearing down everything Pa had done." I saw the change as permission to dance on Sunday. The music changed, with more clapping and rocking as a new Dunbar choir was formed and I was recruited to join. "The Rev. Tucker can't object with his granddaughter in our membership," the Rev. Paul said. I was instructed to sing alto, which the choir leaders told me meant "so low you can't be heard." While I was barely singing I was clearly rocking, as the new choir swayed down the aisle to "Lead Me, Guide Me, Ol' Lord Today."

Pa heard from Mrs. Dasher how I continued to teach Sunday school and usher, but not of my singing or the new choir. Cousin Henry said Pa knew things would be different, "but always in God's hand." Cousin Henry was with Pa when he died at home just a few weeks before my graduation.

The *Afro-American News* gave extensive coverage to his funeral, the many causes he championed as pastor of Union

Baptist Church for 40 years, his pioneer missionary work in Haiti and the many churches he had founded. I understood in reading about him how he established closeness, not in the hugging that I had missed from him, but in bringing people together in a way that protected them from being alone. Grandfather Tucker had learned many things that had not been valued, taught or tested in his schooling. He placed his hope for a better future in the achievements of his people.

I wrote and rewrote my essay as if hope for the future had been placed on me. Grief and love powered me. My essay was selected. At 17, I led my class in the procession and gave my speech with only the smallest trace of a stutter.

MILE 8.3

Just a few more miles to go. Can't be lulled into a trance. Keep pressing forward. There are so many reasons to keep focused. What was that I saw on television this morning about cutbacks in social programs and despair in our communities? Let me remember. Today I'll use the anger to help me run harder and get through these miles.

The voice I used in my speech, like the voice my family used in public, was optimistic and inspirational. But at home, we knew and would speak of lynchings, cross burnings, what had happened to Emmett Till and the Jim Crow laws that continued to humiliate us. We were fearful of what might result from the more strident approaches we observed in protests. On one hand, we were primed to take risks that might endanger us, and on the other, to seek safe routes to protect ourselves, to get on with our lives.

At a job interview with the personnel director at the Newark Board of Education, I noted there were no Negroes in the office, just as my mother had said. I had passed the civil service examination for senior clerk stenographer, and I was seeking a job from a man who many years before had been my Uncle Matthew's Latin teacher. After asking me to take a seat, the personnel director looked at me. "Do you know how to read?" he asked. A stutter filled my throat. He countered my hesitation in answering with a request that I read for him. I read slowly, proudly, yet I felt diminished that my ability to read had been doubted.

I had never been given the impression that whites were fair, but I felt that having done so well on my civil service exams gave me status. And even more, I felt that things were changing; everything was going to be so much better. I was encouraged by the *Brown v. Board of Education* decision, the lunchcounter protests in the South and the bold tones of the voices that spoke out. It was to my thinking just a matter of more of us passing exams, more changes in the legislation, more people moving ahead—and life would be better for our people. Segregated low-income housing projects would be a thing of the past. Ethnic rivalries were blurred by the reality of our competing with the children of immigrants and succeeding. The frog became a metaphor for the world, as we believed our kiss, our embrace, would change our circumstance.

The year 1954 was a turning point for our nation and our family. I got the job at the Board of Education. My mother decided to accept a civil service appointment again as telephone operator in Newark's City Hospital. She had been away from work for four years. Plumper, tougher and more severe, she was relentless in declaring she wouldn't take any stuff from anyone this time. Not only was she "good," she said, "I know my rights and they had better not mess with me." The hint that she would possibly be turned away sent her into a tirade. When I suggested she smile to win her new colleagues over, she laughed and said, "What for?" Her anger was clear. While she was glad to have new opportunities, she didn't seem happier. She still would not talk about her time away or what had pushed her to the breakdown.

At the Board of Education, I was befriended by an older woman, Mrs. Malone, who took to coming in on Saturdays to retype statistical tables for me and telling me what to watch out for in the behavior of others. She was the supportive co-worker that Ma was always looking for. I learned from Mrs. Malone the struggles she endured as an Irish immigrant and realized how rough some poor white families had it. Her wardrobe consisted of two dresses. Once a week she would bring one of the dresses from the cleaners and change in the ladies room. With no children of her own, she advised me as if I were family. She viewed my working as ensuring my independence , just as the Irish had struggled and had been persecuted. Moreover, her "very Catholic" family just did not understand her having to support Mr. Malone and being childless.

Enraged to learn that despite my high school grades I had

never been advised to take college preparatory courses, she urged me to go to college. I found that I could make up credits by taking statewide exams in missed academic units. So I continued working full-time while studying to take the exams to make up four academic units. In the fall of 1954, I began taking courses at Seton Hall University in Newark. I knew, from my first semester, that I wouldn't turn back. I would do what I had to do to matriculate. I saw myself finishing and earning my college degree.

At the same time, I realized I couldn't just drop out of my family and work and go to school. The activities of my mother and sister vied for my attention. My mother was looking for the pefect job that would "suit her," getting started again. My having attained a civil service position, and having scored well in the process, encouraged her. Her daughter's being employed as a senior clerk stenographer signaled that she'd been a good mother. Jean was engaged, and there was a wedding to plan and pay for. I wanted to help finance her wedding. Though it was still a year away, it was a good project for both of us as we thought of ourselves as being close to living "happily ever after."

MILE 9

Running a marathon is about the self, moving with others, yet solitary. You're out there experiencing, being in touch with yourself, with your knowledge of your body, its movement, adaptations and sensitivity. Barring injury, the satisfaction and positive feelings caress your insides, nurture your core as you respond to the heel-toe motion.

There's a natural, uncomplicated feeling of contentment as you settle in to do your best. It's about you, the test you've elected in choosing to run a marathon. You're opposing no one, but rather being with one—yourself. Being in tune is key. You search for that harmony before lining up at the start. "It is going to be all right," you tell yourself. It is about being in the experience, being alive and having this event be a gift you've given yourself.

Running a marathon is about others who choose to run it with you. You're aware of each other, of the space each of you needs to finish. You glide, never pushing, that is, if you understand marathoning. It's about others who pass you and those you leave behind—and always about all of you getting to the finish line. It's wanting the best for those who choose to run the marathon.

Running a marathon is also about the course. You know when you start that it all has to be covered. The flat, less difficult terrain, the rolling or steep hills, the road turns, the gravel, tar or cement pavement—it all has to be covered. Some parts of the run are harder than others and require discipline, focus, will, sheer guts to persevere. You know you have to, want to, get through it and go the distance. The course is to be dealt with wisely. The marathon course is to be respected, as therein lies your soul.

"Blue moon, you saw me standing alone, without a dream in my heart, without a love of my own... da da ... now I'm no longer alone without a love of my own."

I couldn't remember the words, but I was singing and embellishing to anyone who would listen my meeting and

courting and being courted by Tom Cross. I had gone to a blue
light party in East Orange, joined him in conversation on the
couch and danced to a slow song while adjusting to his 6-foot,
10-inch gorgeous to-die-for frame. From Hagerstown,
Maryland, he was attending Seton Hall University on a basketball scholarship. As he spoke I added up all the reasons my
family would like him. He offered what they perceived as
advantages: fair skin, good looks and nice hair. Plus, he was in
college and had a nice voice. There were other pretty East
Orange women at the party but he talked only to me that night.
I learned how he had traveled to Waynesboro, Pennsylvania, to
go to school while living in Hagerstown because the high
schools in Maryland were still segregated. I spoke of my rage
at injustice and strong feelings on the subject of segregation.
We sensed what we might learn from each other. And we
laughed together when he added how he'd been warned about
city women.

I went home and wrote this in my diary about our first
meeting:

> Dear Diary: On the way home in Boo's car, Tom kissed
> me, and worst of all, I let him. I don't know if I just want-
> ed him to kiss me or I was too shocked to hold him off. I
> felt for a while that this Tom is quite bold; should I let
> myself like him? But he looked so gentle, kind and won-
> derful. He asked me for a date to the movies Sunday night
> and I have accepted. When we reached my door, he kissed
> me good night. I should not have let him, and I enjoyed it.

We were both 18, virgins and the first in our families to be
in college, he full-time on scholarship and I full-time while
working days at the Board of Education. I was drawn to him
and his story. He had attended segregated elementary school
classes and earned some money working for whites doing
menial groundskeeping jobs. He had experienced the rejection
of his mother, who gave birth to him out of wedlock. His mother gave him to Mrs. Anna Cross, a widow, to raise with her
grandchildren in a small house on a limited income. His hard-

ships had claimed more of him than mine had of me. But his stature, accident of color and refinement of speech counted, I felt, for something.

I focused on how I could help him by writing and typing his papers and being a resource as he learned the ways of the North. I wanted our friendship to work. He had been told by the guys in school that he could do better with a light-skinned sorority sister from Montclair or East Orange. When we weren't together, I would be waiting for a call from him outside a public telephone booth at a scheduled time. We didn't have a phone at home.

Our courtship did not go unnoticed. Tom received a note from Seton Hall's Father Horgan advising him of the seriousness of staying with his girlfriend over weekends. "The violation is so serious that if it is done the penalty is expulsion from school," Father Horgan said. I responded to his letter: "We cannot see the seriousness of his being our guest and must conclude you imply something morally wrong with his staying here."

The college officials had no idea of the steps my mother was taking to make sure Tom and I didn't go beyond heavy petting and sweating. When Tom spent the night, my mother would put him up in the living room and place her bed in the hallway separating my room from the living room. Nor could they imagine the depth of the lectures Tom would receive from my uncles on the importance of finishing school and not getting too serious. And there was the pressure of his teammates to keep his mind on the game.

I was angered most by the school's reaction to our dating. They weren't in touch with the pressures real to him. Nor did they deal with the impact on Tom of playing games in the South and being segregated in lodging from his teammates. Yet I also worried about the school's disapproval of our relationship and the potential effect on his scholarship.

We were both confronted with new opportunities at a time when the world appeared to be opening like a giant rose. We were left to mentor each other as our families wished us well and imagined we'd been embraced and expected to be where we were. Tom and I were buoyed by the times. Nothing could stop us. Segregation would be ending. Our families were strong. If we could just get through this tough time, over this hurdle, life would get better. The sacrifices would pay off.

We could be together all the time if we were married, so we decided on a small church wedding in Hagerstown in the summer before the next school year started. I modified the dress Jean wore at her wedding and added a new tiara.

We enjoyed the support of both of our families, who agreed I could help Tom get through school. While I wanted to finish college too, I would not let my going obstruct what we had for Tom. Tom continued to receive $10 a week from school and was not expected to work beyond practice for the team. In the fall after we were married, I had to put a stop payment on the check I'd given to pay my college tuition. I arranged to be at the bank when it opened and stuttered badly as I explained to the bank clerk. Tears filled my eyes as I completed the necessary forms.

The semester before I had earned placement on the dean's list, and while I had proudly shared that achievement, I would not tell my family of having to drop out. My family saw me as taking risks, not being satisfied with what I had in my job at the Board of Education and the good luck I had in marrying Tom Cross. I didn't want to hear from them about what I couldn't do and the boundaries I should set on expectations for myself. Going the distance for them meant my being close to the family and taking the necessary steps to secure my marriage. They appreciated the value of my college experience as a help in the marriage. I was in a sense participating in the revolution by ensuring Tom's success and being a partner in his learning. I embraced the role, serving and saying, "It's gonna be all right," as I'd seen my grandmother, Aunt Jean and Mrs. Malone do. I saw myself exhibiting the strength I'd seen in my mother, yet I didn't want to lose myself, as I had seen her lose herself in getting sick. When the money got tight I added a second job to my full-time work.

But I secretly held the idea of achieving more for myself. I wanted to serve as I had seen my uncles serve as leaders in the community with a passion about improving the condition for Negroes. And I wanted to be like my grandfather in having the time to do missionary work in Haiti. Did other women secretly share my views on leading as well as nurturing? What happened if they revealed their suppressed thoughts? Our girl talk focused on what our dream house would look like, how many children we wanted and our consciousness of the influence of skin color on access to our dreams. I couldn't fathom the lives or conversations of young women my age who went to college full-time, lived in residence halls and participated in clubs and sororities. Nor could I imagine how a young married woman spent her time or what she talked about if she were home without a job and being taken care of by her husband.

I learned about sex and procreation in sound bites: "Make sure he wears something" and "She's late." I read books on the menstrual cycle and counted for the safe days. I was in disbelief when in the spring of 1957 my period didn't come. Waiting and folding into tears again and again, I tried to abort with laxatives and sheer will. Tom cried too, but he talked of all the things we had succeeded in doing to this point. The pregnancy for us, he said, would be another challenge. He'd work that summer at a can company, and I would work from home in addition to my full-time job. Above all, Tom would continue on his basketball scholarship and complete his education. There was never question of his stopping school.

We marveled at the feel of the baby kicking, taking its own time to make an appearance. We hoped for a boy as our first-born and the first grandchild in both our families. Despite the fullness of the baby, I felt an emptiness and anxiousness that was temporarily relieved by eating. I made regular excursions to the new Dunkin' Donuts chain store near us for two to a half-dozen treats at a time. I craved Ritz crackers.

At some point in the middle of the pregnancy, however, I began to view my state as a project by which we were being judged. I imagined people wondering, "Will they be able to make it with a child? Will having a baby obstruct his plans?" I worried about being viewed as a liability to Tom. While I was clearly pregnant and struggling with an ever-expanding girth, we didn't even talk about the baby with friends. Our conversations were of Tom's achievements on the basketball court and his papers and exams.

At the same time, my mother was in the middle of a lawsuit. She had been denied the position of supervisor in her civil service job even though she ranked first on the list. The job had been given to a white woman who ranked second. When it became clear she had been passed over, Ozie hired a lawyer to take her case to the state office in Trenton. Daily she shared her frustration with us about trying to get her lawyer to follow up the initial filing. In her visits to our apartment, she spread out her files of letters and read them to us. I felt her determination and strength, yet I worried about the impact of the proceedings on her. She wasn't going to be distracted from her fight to become a mellow grandparent.

I continued to work full-time and type student papers at home until a few weeks before childbirth. I had gained 50 pounds. In labor, I felt my face stretch as I screamed in pain until I passed out. I awakened to the music of the words, "You have a 9-pound, 6-ounce beautiful baby boy, Tom Cross Jr."

I returned to work seven weeks later in a fog that was both labeled and dismissed as postpartum depression. It was to linger and linger. I was told that the blues were to be "endured" like cramps during menses. I was consciously aware of trying not to project my state or the baby's presence as a burden.

Most days, I would leave my job at the Board of Education, return home to fix dinner for Tom and the two students who lived with us and paid board. Then I would spend some time with Tom Jr. and take the bus downtown to evening classes. My lunch hours were spent studying and typing papers for both of us. At night, when I was not in school, I would read to Tom Jr. from my textbooks, changing the inflection and grimacing and smiling. Tom, as well as other students, would care for Tommy between classes. During exams we found someone to come in until I returned home. Nothing would stop us, we thought.

And while my mother would come over and repeatedly caution us about letting too many people into our lives— "Keep your business to yourself"—we created a family with our student friends. My mother was the last to know about our house parties, where we'd laugh and talk of our struggles to stay on track. We would debate about religion and whether Brooklyn or Harlem was the center of the universe. Our parties were dry until we realized that the absence of liquor was causing our friends to run out to their cars for a swig or leave early. At 21, I had never had a drink nor been particularly curious about what I was missing.

Tom's being a student and basketball player were paramount. One night, we were thrilled when his picture made the cover of the program at Madison Square Garden and devastated when Oscar Robertson scored an all-time high of 61 points against Seton Hall in the game. I worried that in trying to save money by serving chicken instead of steak for his pre-game dinner, I had caused the disaster.

The pressures were enormous. Tom had to meet expectations on the basketball court and maintain an acceptable grade point average with his French major and Spanish minor. In failing to heed advisors who had urged him to take a less rigorous route to a degree, we had lost some support. In choosing to go ahead, we were defying the stereotypes of him as an athlete who could not also be a scholar.

We prided ourselves on not being new to a struggle and on being very much in line with the spirit of defiant demonstrations erupting in the late 1950s. We managed to stay afloat financially by moving frequently to lower our rent costs or to find an apartment large enough to accommodate student tenants. I had mastered the creation and cooking of every kind of casserole imaginable to make the most of our budget for food. I was intent in showing that I had the ability to be instrumental in our success. Yearning to return to school, however, I had to figure out how and when I could do it.

Tom's first cousin, Alice, and her postal worker husband, Paul, were there to affirm that through believing in myself, I could earn my degree. Ten years my senior, with hazel eyes and smooth brown skin, Alice was a beautiful woman who was skilled in cooking and sewing. She created beauty herself, fulfilling her dreams for the good fortune of her children and husband. Alice was quick and clear in telling me that Tom's family should be falling at my feet with joy that I was there to help and provide the support that Tom needed. "Dee, you and I are both Virgos, meaning we're creative, resourceful, persistent and hard workers who make things happen. The key is to believe in yourself, in magic, and to dream and recreate your environment to match your spirit." Our drives from our home in East Orange to their home in Willow Grove took us to her world of make-believe turned to reality. A former prom queen and an only child, she had been taught by her mother, Catherine, to create a glorious Never-Never Land out of what at first glance looked liked a small, quite ordinary house. It was a home, welcoming with flowers, plants and antiques and the rocking chair where she would hold her babies and take them to new places with her plans. Karann was the oldest, caught in her mother's dreams of her as Sleeping Beauty, a dream Alice captured in a mural of the prince, poised to waken Sleeping Beauty, painted on the wall in Karann's bedroom. And then there was young Pat, his legs in braces as he struggled to walk in a family that saw his braces as all quite temporary, and young Allie tugging at his mother. Alice created a place where all of them thrived by doing what she dreamed of.

Tom's fifth and final year at Seton Hall in 1958-59 was the toughest and most challenging. He was co-captain of the basketball team. Furthermore, he had to complete his student teaching and the credentials process and begin the awesome project of securing a teaching job. It meant getting through a maze of paperwork, piecing information together and finding a direction.

We were optimistic even though the news around us was

not promising. Dinah Washington's untimely death in the segregated Sahara Hotel in 1959 and the upholding of pupil placement laws in 17 states affected by the *Brown* decision were
blows to progress. We nonetheless naively felt that our credentials and achievements would lessen the fury of racism.

In seeking a job, Tom would find the same pattern: an initial intrigue with his height, his bilingualism and stories of his
days on the basketball court and then—nothing. We learned
what happens when there is no mentor, advocate or anyone
interested in your success off the court. Yet we continued to
feel we were ahead.

I returned to being a student full time in the evenings in
the spring of 1960. I carried five college courses, having completed my high school academic deficiencies in the sciences
and algebra. Our household included Ray Proctor, a student
who continued to live with us after his graduation. Ray was
flamboyant and charismatic, challenging me with great fervor
about what he felt was my having resigned myself to an instrumental role in the marriage. I didn't feel Tom was comfortable
with Ray's urging me to step out and do my thing, but everything he said endeared him to me. Tom's young cousin Steven
Tyler also moved in with us from Hagerstown. We were told he
was proving to be too difficult for his mother to raise. When he
was not with us, Steve would stay with my sister Jean, her husband, Jake, and their daughter, Karen. Our lives were full.

Jane was born before I completed my undergraduate
studies. I was close to delivering her in August 1962, the summer of Tom's Fulbright studies in Puerto Rico, before Ray even
acknowledged I was pregnant and moved out to give us the
space we needed.

I had prayed that Jane would come early so we might gain
the benefit of another stipend for dependents. The night my
water broke, I felt that the baby within me and God had coop-
erated to get us through another tough financial time. The
pains were even stronger than I'd remembered in giving birth
to Tommy. I was exhausted by Jane's birth, which came on top
of working non-stop, going to school, caring for Tom Jr., man-

aging a home with tenants, and following up on what needed to be done as Tom applied for certification and teaching positions, but I was awed by our baby girl.

Jane was healthy, beautiful, and in my mind, perfect. She was fair like her father in complexion and had light brown hair. I perceived she would have advantages in a world that viewed people of deep color as threatening. Her light complexion would help her for her whole life. At the same time I also felt inadequate and intimidated by her advantages. What could she need from me? What could I add, given these advantages? I held her close on that first day home and then passed her to Tom. I sank into a chair and stayed for what seemed like hours fighting the fright of being both awed and overwhelmed. I was close to completing my undergraduate degree, but there were so many other concerns vying for my attention. Uppermost in my mind was the need to complete my own requirements for teaching credentials and at the same time remain financially solvent.

It had been eight years since I started taking courses. I finally completed what was required for a degree in elementary education by teaching kindergarten full-time for a year at Fifteenth Avenue School. The assignment meant I could take Tom Jr., also a kindergartner, with me when his school was closed. My co-teacher, Lena, was an excellent first teaching partner, a descendant of Polish royalty (or so she said). She was a free spirit who just happened to have collaborated in the hit song "Monster Mash." Lena encouraged my eccentricities, and together we sought outlandish approaches to our appearance and our teaching to captivate the attention of our kindergartners. I shared with her how I was learning to have fun just playing and she shared with me her ideas about what it meant to be royal: "Having someone pick up the panties you step out of and leave on the floor." I'd go home and do just that. What a luxurious experience for me, if not for Tom.

Graduation came at the end of my first year of teaching. With Jane in tow, the family attended my graduation. My mother managed to find and wear the widest black brim hat I had ever seen. She did not conceal her joy, as she regarded my diploma as her trophy.

Even as I received my diploma, I knew that succeeding meant putting what was taught in school in perspective. We all were urged in school to compete, yet to survive we had to cooperate with each other and the extended families we formed. Schools would stress that most of our energy should be directed to the development of the mind, yet to succeed we had to grow in those vulnerable areas of love, pain, sorrow and other precious emotions. Schools were still dealing with clear delineations of male and female roles, yet to succeed we had to share roles. Schools were regarding blacks as entering as blank slates. To succeed we knew we had to draw upon what we learned from our parents, what we knew of our ancestors and what we had experienced in our extended families. And while schools promoted the individual, we knew to succeed that we had to think in terms of community.

The talk and music of the 1960s were arousing and convincing. "Come on, baby, let's do the twist." We moved as we hadn't moved before, twisting and turning, having fun, yet so intense, focused on moving up as well as around. Stairs seemed to appear for us to ascend. We speculated about what would be there once we reached one level. Could we rest and reflect? Or would we have to keep going up another flight, and yet another?

MILE 10

"We shall overcome. We shall overcome. We shall overcome some da-a-ay." Listen to your breathing and hit your stride. Accelerate. Lift your legs. Get some spring. Move it.

We turned up the car radio to hear the leaders one by one speak to the marchers. We listened as the world listened. Tom Jr., 6, and Jane, 2, sat quietly in the back seat responding to our firm shushing and our distraction as we were pulled by the magnetic voice filling the car.

"I have a dream. I have a dream that the sons of former slaves and the sons of former slave owners will be able to sit together at the table of brotherhood."

We were working to make that dream real as we moved from East Orange to Hempstead, Long Island, just as people engaged in the March on Washington. We never stopped but looked ahead to the cars and road before us, scanning the signs for exit 19 on the Southern State Parkway.

It would be different for our children in Hempstead. We had already checked out opportunities for them as we acknowledged the mix of things for them to do as they got ready for their places at the table. We floated on the optimism of the March just as we were jarred when three weeks after the March, four young girls were killed in the Birmingham, Alabama, church bombing.

At home and with friends we would talk about how to do it all: how to find and keep our jobs in integrated places; how to prepare our children for integrated places; how to make a statement about our very deep feelings about our rights; how to handle the rage that sprang from our youth; and how to maintain a reasonable approach to taking risks, given our responsibility to our children.

Doing it all included responding to social issues in a way that involved us all. We were not going to be rejected After living for 18 months in Hempstead, we challenged whites who refused to show and sell houses to blacks. We'd go through the humiliating experience of being turned away and being regarded with disdain. We'd watch as the occupant of a house peered through the blinds and avoided answering the door. We attended meetings with whites who had received a different response—a welcome—when they tested the same houses.

In 1965 we purchased our first home and moved to Lakeview, New York. Our colonial-style house faced a pond and was framed with trees. We were attentive to what we had, painting and repairing our home and blending into our progressive, largely black community in Lakeview. We were as parents aware of the pain, the possibilities and the promises of the 1960s. My Lakeview neighbors became our extended family. We were brought together when the schools were ordered to desegregate. The nearby Malverne schools were virtually all white, while those in Lakeview were increasingly black. The efforts to integrate the two systems were being resisted by the whites in Malverne at a time when the black families in Lakeview were united in our expectation for fairer treatment of our children and an improved education. We did not intend to compromise. We were buoyed by the work of black authors and leaders: James Baldwin, Leroy Jones, Malcolm X and Martin Luther King. We wore dashikis and natural Afros and celebrated the whole idea of "Black is Beautiful."

We were grounded by our visits with Alice and Paul and their family, going on picnics and to the World's Fair in Queens, New York. We would dream with Alice and Paul about the world we'd open up for our children. Alice brought her cherry pies to our house and took over my kitchen, never once chiding me for my lack of culinary skills. Instead, she listened for my accomplishments, marveling that I had found time to strip and paint the furniture and the fireplace and install shutters in the kitchen, while working full-time, attending graduate school at night and commuting one hour to my job in Brentwood.

We also joined Jack and Jill for social events and took trips to the theatre in Manhattan. And I spent time getting to know other mothers in the neighborhood, sharing the usual talk about homework and yard sales. Despite all of Alice's suggestions that I stop and smell the roses, mostly I was distracted by the political realities of Malverne.

On weekdays we'd meet and prepare for demonstrations in Malverne on the weekends. We would join with our children, neighbors and friends to hold hands and sing "We Shall Overcome" or hold a silent vigil. Arguing about strategy, we lamented that some blacks held back or even seemed bent on betraying us.

I was 29. Forty was old, and I wondered if, given the stress and the pace, I would live to see 40. Would I burn out or be taken out by the violence of racism? I was frightened by my willingness to die, if the sacrifice would have made things better, for my people. The *Brown* decision a little more than a decade before seemed a century old. I was angry and scared for my children. I had seen the hatred in the eyes of the whites who fought integration of the Malverne schools. The madness was overwhelming. These were my children. We had paid our dues, made sacrifices, given up so much. How dare they! How dare they! Yet the insults kept coming.

When Jane was five, she left the babysitter's house when the sitter wasn't looking and set out for our home a block and a half away. She let herself in through the back door and wandered up and down the stairs crying and looking for me. But I was off trying to make her future better. Her sitter found her and took her back.

I found some consolation in reading black history stories to my children. I wanted them to know what we had achieved as a people. We traced the journey from Africa to these shores, speaking both of the horrors of slavery and the strength of the slaves, how they communicated and suffered to be free. Late one evening, I asked Jane to sum up in a sentence what she understood from my readings. She answered, "Mommy, it's different. Now they pay the slaves." I found myself repeating her response while carrying on the simplest of tasks, driving, cleaning, shopping. I could not shake it. And I began to think about what real change would look like.

The summer before Jane was to start classes in Malverne, we went into the district school where she was tested. I beamed as the teacher went on and on about how well Jane had tested, grades ahead of her peers. When the session was over, we went outside where white parents had gathered, chanting and frowning at our presence. I held on to Jane's hand and walked as my mother had shown me years ago how to walk on dark nights in Newark. I told Jane she was a princess. We carried ourselves royally. They would not see me cringe. I was angry at the knowledge that I had not walked my child into better times. What would it mean for her to be ahead of her peers? Would her difference be appreciated any more than mine had been? How real were the barriers? I felt anxious.

We had to keep pushing. When the district agreed to integrate the schools but drew the line on providing busing, I took the lead in organizing the Lakeview Self Help Group to manage our own busing. Gwen Whiten and I collected money from our Lakeview neighbors, rented buses and mapped a bus route. We kept the buses going for months until the district took over the route.

In an April 1968 letter to the Malverne Teachers Association, Tom and I expressed our frustration and challenged their resistance to integration efforts. Many of them had advised us in our efforts, but they never spoke up about what was right. "At our personal expense and our personal humiliation, we bussed our kindergarten and third grade children, while we afforded integration without inconvenience for the young whites of Malverne and Lynbrook. Since the sacrifice of Dr. King, we wonder if the price was too high and too compromising. It is a question we must answer. Did we bow down again? With our consciences and our experiences, we are pessimistic about the impact of an open letter. You have made the first step, but you need the leadership, courage and commitment to do so much more."

We then focused on the integration of the high school and planned a demonstration. It was my job to get into the building, stage a distraction and open the front door to let the demonstrators inside the building. It was a risk I took, one that might have had severe consequences. As the others marched into the school I walked home slowly, stunned by where my rage had taken me. I couldn't fully enjoy my triumph. I was aware—painfully so—that with each step there was more to do to make a difference.

I began to question if my views on equity were compatible with my teaching in special education classes. I could not escape the impact of blackness on who was put into those classes. The placement of black children into special education classes seemed to me a by-product of integration. When traditional institutions could not or would not absorb a population, they called in the "specialists" in special education. The specialists, though noble in heart, lobbied for more like them and began to over-identify blacks for these special classes. In my observation, all too often nothing special was happening. I saw younger and older black children being viewed as sick when at times they were rebelling appropriately at the absurdities imposed by adults. This was happening disproportionately to young black boys.

At the same moment when we were working to do the right thing in the passion of the 1960s, the contradictions edged close to home. One day, we received a call from Tom Jr.'s teacher. The teacher had discovered items in Tommy's desk that had been missing. He felt a "referral" was appropriate. By "referral" he meant psychological testing. Tommy's grades didn't seem to matter; it looked to the teacher that he had an "emotional problem." I was in the teacher's face the next day, raising questions about what had happened so I could hear him recount what he had discovered in Tom's desk. I asked that Tommy be brought in from the playground so I could hear from him directly what had happened. Tommy explained how he had been asked by his classmates to store the materials in his desk. He was the butt of a class joke. I was sickened by the reality that the teacher had not asked Tom to explain the circumstances but rather had chosen to see the incident as the criminal behavior of a young black male. I was furious.

I shared my observations with Gabe Simches, my supervisor in the Brentwood Public Schools. Fully aware of the racism directed against blacks, Gabe related his experiences as a Jew growing up in New York. Until Gabe, I had never met a white person ready to go to war against white racists. He was in touch with the depth of their depravity. I confessed to him that while I was involved in the civil rights movement, I did not expect change. He was more optimistic, noting how he and I and others on the right side of the issue had already changed. But I wasn't comforted by things merely changing. Despite all the energy we had expended, we still confronted resistance. Championing change, I was nonetheless painfully aware of my doubts and uncomfortable about where such doubts could take me. I had to move ahead and deal with realities I wanted to deny.

Our discussion happened as the 14 special education students in my classroom swirled about us. We were caught in this intense, unexpected exchange of views. Gabe countered my thoughts with what he viewed as successes. For instance, his friend George, a black male, had obtained the level of achievement of mutual friends in acquiring a home in all-white Baldwin. Plus, there were successes at the polls in the North and South.

It was impossible to communicate to him that despite all of that, I didn't foresee a time to rest. I couldn't imagine society expecting me to succeed and accepting me as a creative spirit. We were, as a family, all dressed up with no place to go, but with much to do. We had defied the odds, struggled to complete our degrees and hold our family together, yet with each step forward, something tried to convince me that we were running in place.

I had played my role as being instrumental in our marriage and in the community, in the spirit I'd seen in other women in my family. It was a role in which you clearly defined your husband as the center. I'd done well in marrying. Yet the bottom was falling out, as Tom struggled to keep teaching jobs in largely white school districts.

Things would start out well. They liked his height, his good looks, his good diction and his having availed himself of a Fulbright award. Again and again, however, we saw a lack of interest in his success.

It had been barely ten years since black males had reached the job heights of being employed in the post office or as Pullman porters. The integration of the 1960s did not mean acceptance for blacks in jobs where there had been figurative and literal white-only designations.

At home at night I would vent my rage about his experience, hoping to get him angry, to get him to the point of protesting, taking a militant posture. I knew in the end we'd resolve the situation by moving on, to another place to try again. He listened as I communicated my despair, replying, "It all doesn't matter." I tried to convince myself that with his love, nothing else should matter. But it didn't work. He represented strength to our children, letting them be young while guiding them on how to proceed. He was subjected to the stereotypes held of athletes. No matter what he achieved, most often he heard, "How's the weather up there?" He could be angry without the pain showing.

With resolution, he had defined the "revolution" quite simply as our staying together as a family, as I traveled heavily with the troubles of the world in our luggage. We were aware of our mistakes of wanting all the rewards to come quickly, evidenced in our overspending and financial woes. We filled the void, the emptiness with things, and we hoped to get caught up. We reached out for affirmation from family, and they encouraged our success. We made things happen for each other and for our children to quell the pain of discrimination and rejection. I'd search for new opportunities, new trails to blaze. We'd always, always, convince ourselves that somebody was watching.

MILE II

I run up to the start, glancing around to determine I am the only black and only woman over 50 joining this group of runners at the resort. A male runner runs up to me. (Am I imagining his trying to intercept me?) He blurts out, in earshot of the others, "You're probably looking for the beginners. They're starting on the left of the field." I roll my head, loosen my shoulders, relax and assure him that I haven't made a mistake. I see others look at each other, a check, and then the group moves to begin a two-mile run up an incline. The leader and the group charge out, running faster than they should given the heat and the usual practice of starting out slow. I feel with some amusement and disappointment that these guys and gals are trying to lose me. I won't permit it. I push, centered, taking small steps, using my arms as I charge ahead with intensity and focus. I see the lead runner glance back, checking, challenging. I keep up. I see their sweat, hear them panting. I carry the thought that this run belongs to me. I will not be denied my place nor will I be "put in my place."

Somehow the news reports in the 1960s suggested to me that blacks were on the fringe, not caught up as the liberal whites in the reshaping and redefining of America. In the minds of some we were passive as others were acting to free us. Too often our struggles, our gains, were not recognized as examples of courage as America profiled its heroes and applauded the contributions of enlightened white liberals. There was little evidence in the books I read to my children of our being integral to the success of the country. With events moving so quickly in the 1960s it felt to me that our children would not know, as I had known from my grandparents, "how we had gotten over." We didn't seem to have the time or the gatherings to talk about the past. The present was filled with worry about the disproportionate number of black men being drafted to fight in Vietnam, the turning back of our children as we sought to integrate the schools and the struggles of having to affirm our readiness for a chance at postsecondary education. We were so intent on not being denied our place, that some of us were convinced ourselves that we would be viewed as advanced and prepared to go the distance with the best of them.

We had to keep our lives on course. But we viewed the unrest in our cities and communities as necessary and a telling of our frustration with racism.

One door closed and we'd knock on another. Tom changed jobs several times, moving from Nanuet to East Islip to Roosevelt. He achieved a Fulbright scholarship to study in Spain the summer of 1967. He was gone when the riots broke out in Newark. Jane and Tom Jr. were visiting with my mother. When I called, she asked me not to travel to pick them up and promised she would keep them inside her apartment, which was in earshot of the noise and looting. I called every hour and worried deeply as my mother spoke "of the revolution in Newark" and her view that it was important for the children to be in Newark at what she viewed as an historic moment that in the end would be positive. She fathomed that somehow the country would learn of the inequities for blacks and the conditions of the poor. I knew as she spoke she was also referring to her own story. She spent every available moment researching her case about being passed over for the civil service position while she continued her education at Union College. She viewed the riot as a display of rage, her own included.

My letters to Tom in Spain were filled with concern about making ends meet and the riots in Newark. I shared how many had died and how I learned that our friends Dan and Sally had been stoned in their car in the white area of Vailsburg. I wrote of the deeper militance in Sally's voice and her comments that she felt safer in her ghetto, given the hostility in the heart of Newark. The National Guard and police ransacked many homes looking for rifles. A newsman was arrested for filming the National Guard destroying property. I saved the articles about the riots, agreeing with my mother that, considering the unresolved conflicts from my school days in Newark, the world should not have been surprised. I abhorred the politicians who attempted to dismiss it all under the banner of "criminal behavior and subversion in America," while making no comment on the horrors of poverty. The distortion angered me deeply, as did the contradictions in our lives. Our young family was intent on defying the odds. By being the first generation in our families to attend college, we were preparing to serve with distinction and in the process contribute to the view that helping others like us has merit for society. But the riots imprinted on the minds of many a view of blacks as dangerous. The mood of the country was disconnected from the achievements of aspiring blacks and their families and friends.

In 1967, we saw, on one hand, the positive impact of the Higher Education Act, which authorized financial aid for college, and, on the other, the proliferation of anti-riot bills and talk of riots as the work of an organized conspiracy. My mother viewed the riots as a catharsis for black folk and the beginning of reconstruction and renewal, while others in my family experienced it quite differently.

My uncle Sam, deeply involved in the politics of Newark, was expected as a "Negro" moderate to help control the situation. Bemoaning the destruction he witnessed in Newark, he felt we were destroying our neighborhoods. He often stopped his car to talk to young people, but they dismissed him. To his thinking, the "new Newarkers," immigrants of color, knew and cared little about what Negro families had contributed to a changing Newark. The powerlessness that Negroes felt could be rectified by voting, he maintained, citing as an example the success Italians had experienced in controlling Newark. He believed in patronage, benefited from patronage and felt it was a means to equity.

Yet as he listened to the reaction of whites, he openly feared that we were being set up for economic suppression. For the first time, he talked about how he'd like to get my Aunt Jean away from Newark, move away as he'd seen his brother

Frank do. Yet we knew from his work in the community that it was not likely to happen. In the months after the riots, I saw him, a man still in his 50s, begin to slow down. He had faced the fires of the human heart and watched neighborhoods turn to cinder. Aunt Jean worried about their personal future as he made his "loans" to help others. She persisted in creating in their small apartment a nest of elegance in pinks and blues, while not far away other homes and businesses had been destroyed.

To most of the world they and the other black residents of Newark were invisible. Other people seemed to me to be caught up in the TV world of "Petticoat Junction," "Dream Girl '67" and "Bonanza." The Newark Uncle Sam and Aunt Jean loved was a fast blur across the TV screens of America.

I commuted from Long Island to work in Harlem in the summer of 1967. So many black men between 25 and 60 seemed just to be sitting around Harlem. Why, with all the antipoverty programs, were there so few for black men? When I returned home each day, Tom and I explained our busy lives of consequence to our children and spoke of the meaning of our efforts. Drawing on the strengths of the Lakeview extended family, we managed to find experiences that would engage them. Yet there was a continuing conflict. I felt the recklessness of being caught up in the revolution when I was summoned home from work that summer of 1967 to learn that Tommy had jumped into the deep end of the swimming pool and almost drowned. In his first swimming lesson, he wanted to become a real swimmer to gain the attention of his friends and perhaps his parents. As I hurried home to him, I was overwhelmed by a myriad of thoughts. I could hear my Aunt Jean saying, "Your children didn't ask to come into this world." But balancing my real guilt was an awareness that like other women in my childhood—my mother and grandmothers Tucker and Johnson—I was living not for myself, but for all the black women who protected their children with prayers as they "made do" for their families and communities. I learned from these women that having children didn't mean you didn't have to work hard outside the home and didn't mean you had to stop improving yourself. I knew not to expect to be petted, put on a pedestal, because I was a woman. These women approached marriage not to get someone to protect them, but to find respect for the nature of their contribution. I seriously felt that continuing their struggle and mine would totally wipe me out by age 40. I could not fathom living until age 50, given what the times demanded of me as a daughter, mother, wife, advocate and black woman intent on defining my life's work as I saw fit. Keeping up would not be without cost.

MILE 12

I have seen people with runner's legs and listened to them talk about the steps they had taken to get that strength. They said they were motivated by others' successes and their awareness of what can happen to your body and mind if you're not taught to be strong or if there is no one interested in your going the distance.

I think about this as I center each footstep on the ground covered with fresh snow. Passing trees trimmed in white, I round Lake Calhoun in the fourth mile of what will be a six-mile run. I'm brushing snow from my eyelids. From my quads to my calves, all I can feel is muscle. I don't want to lose that.

Mirror, mirror on the wall in Newark and in Harlem. I saw my face and the faces of others who struggled to keep their spirits and avoid becoming captives of our curious history. My Hofstra University graduate internship in the spring of 1968, as a principal in a high school for emotionally disturbed adolescents, meant that I traveled daily to a locked-down facility to work with youngsters who "did not adjust" to foster home placement and had no place to go except this wing of Creedmoor Mental Institution in Queens, New York. My supervisor said, "Don't worry, you will mellow about it all as you grow older." But the suggestion that I would reach a point in life when the pain of others didn't matter was frightening.

Lisa, age 16, made the pain clear. "We all in here cause we ugly. Ain't a pretty one here. Nobody likes ugly children. The few white ones are pimply and we black ones are too black and ugly. Am I right? Nobody gonna teach us anything. We gonna stay as we are." I felt strong enough to work with her and to challenge the team of therapists delving into her past, uncovering her wounds, studying her and getting ready to abandon her once they'd written up her case. There were days when I could not separate myself from Lisa. She had been in and out of various foster homes and shunned by other students. A victim of incest from the age of eight, she had been unprotected for most of her young life. She told me that she had to move toward people sexually to avoid hostility. Sometimes she had to fight when she didn't want to. She said she felt safer in the state hospital. On one occasion Lisa shocked me by pulling out a needle and threading it through her thigh, saying without tears, "I feel no pain."

Her troubles mirrored mine in kind, but not degree. Her oppression was so much deeper. My sessions with Lisa focused on what she would need to know to take care of herself, to be strong. We reviewed want ads in the newspaper and talked about what different jobs would entail in skills, dress and attitude. I spoke to her of the importance of finding her life's work and achieving economic independence. At the same time, the research team at the hospital was refusing to honor Lisa's instincts about how the world saw her. They simply weren't doing what was needed to make her strong. The hypocrisy left me spinning and enraged. No one cared about her or poor blacks in general. I felt then I would always be at odds with white institutions that failed to see the validity of a different perspective, a black perspective on the realities of the human condition.

I was committed to staying in touch with what I was learning from Lisa. She trusted what she saw of institutions. She trusted her observations and her instincts and she knew that while she trusted me, what I could do was limited. In a sense, I felt that Lisa knew what was happening to her better than I perhaps knew what was happening to me. I had no response when, in what was our last time together at Creedmore, she said, "They're studying me, but how is that going to help me? I can't change how I look."

When the internship ended, I put space between my graduate experience, with all its contradictions, by walking the five miles from Hofstra University home to Lakeview. I needed the time to deal with feelings I expressed in my diary:

This school pays its dues to the kingdom of "Like it is" perpetuates "Like it Is" and reinforces half-assed egos to accept "Like it is." It's gray in architectural design, personality and commitment. Put within these grey rocks, a black has no standing when she is angry, fairly bright but believes that within a reasonable length of time, a black will emerge who realizes her perspective.

To be black here means you forget that you might be regarded as a welfare recipient, if you are not properly dressed or fail to flash your credentials. Despite it all you adapt so you can change the field (not realizing that nobody gray through and through has ever played the game with an intent to change it fairly). You imagine a team, academic in orientation, with noble views to save the world and you. You forget that blacks are dreamers and are courted these days because they are dreamers. There is no more cotton to be picked so black thoughts are picked and their dreams are revealed so that gray humanity can feign saving humanity. You look at the Afro hair-dos of young blacks and feel their light stuff compared to the real upside-down changes they are making inside, the many times they play the scene "Like it Is." What waste, futility, despair, frustration and stark desperation.

To be black here means you fight for the underdog; fight what is unjust, take on a cause. It doesn't have to be your cause, but you're in prime mood and your blackness is put to work to generate fear and make the whole damn spoof look good. Grays need the fear you generate for simple, simple, simple, stupid courage. And so I say "boo" eloquently. And, as a black, I am subject to the brain drain, scrub-up, tacky job, and expected to fight on—no matter how high the crap piles up—you march on singing, "we shall overcome." I do my thing, child of the depression, protege of the fairy tales and believer. That is, until I wake up with my mind "stayed on freedom" because I want to save my mind for something a hell of a lot better, maybe a revolution. That is, if I have the courage to look into the line of fire rather than away. Damn, being gray may be contagious.

To be black here and to stay here, and not stretch out, is to be an ass. It is like this: Slavery is still expected. When you're fairly intelligent—it is read—you're a good nigger. The virtues of the black are discussed as if preparing the slave for market. Grays take the credit for a job well done. And it's beautiful having blacks working for you. When push comes to shove you can get what you need and act like they were never there. Because to grays, I wasn't there.

What's the purpose of this diary entry? A silent protest, still my stupid style, imagining I can cause a sleepless night for a gray. It's my aggression. My knife (this pen) assumes there's a sensitivity to a person, rather than a vacancy on the plantation.

The crushing weight of the 1960s fell on black people. Inequities persisted in housing, education and job opportunities. We were meant to be role models leading change and inspiring change, while not missing a beat in all aspects of our lives. We were meant to keep looking forward, adapting as if the healing was happening and we had indeed achieved some exclusive benefits. We had to make adjustments in light of the familiar patterns of rejection and new opportunities that might lead to acceptance.

About the same time my stint at the Hofstra Graduate School was coming to a close, two events happened simultaneously that changed our course. Tom learned that his teaching contract might not be renewed. And he saw an ad for "Head Advisor, Brown Hall, Eastern Michigan University," complete with an apartment, board and a salary. We saw a chance to start again. Tom would apply to the University of Michigan to study for a doctorate and I would have the job of head advisor at the hall in Ypsilanti, Michigan. We could sell our house in Lakeview and deal with our mounting debt while saving face. We made the decision sound great to our family and friends. And we worked hard to convince our children that the experience would lead to more adventures. We distributed to family and friends all the furniture our new apartment would not take. And on our last night at 3 Colonial Road, I cried in Tom's arms and felt his tears too. Though I was in his arms, I felt alone and let down. We had reached maturity with strong wills and ancestry, yet our instincts were so tender.

There had been nights when I had lain awake and wondered how different the life we were living was than the life experienced by my parents. Had it gotten better? My children might say that their parents had entered history before most homes had telephones and televisions and when living in the housing projects was regarded as moving to Sugar Hill. And they would reflect that while their mother had attended integrated elementary schools, their father had not. As parents, we were passionate, reckless even, in our efforts to protect our children from being denied opportunity because of the color of their skin. And it was clear in those fitful nights that discrimination haunted us just as it did my parents.

MILE 13

Every part of my body tells me I should have stretched, taken the time to warm my muscles. But I had things to do.

I can't lose ground. I'm out here doing it but not enjoying today's run. Lift it up, push ahead, whew, breathe, almost there, such a heaviness. Not much fun, but it's out of the way. My hip is feeling it. I should have stretched and listened to my body.

The summer before our move to Michigan, Tom accepted the position of assistant principal at Ypsilanti Junior High School and decided not to pursue a doctorate, but rather an educational specialist in administration degree at the University of Michigan. We were committed to the new direction but we hadn't prepared ourselves for life in Brown Hall. I had come in as the first black woman head advisor in a racially divided situation. It was the first time many of the white women students had gone to school with, let alone lived with, black women. And the black women from Detroit and Benton Harbor weren't going to take any stuff, especially with a black woman head advisor and her family on board. I was thrust into the role of being, at 32, a parent to 212 women at Brown Hall, as well as handling all the adjustment problems that Jane and Tommy had in moving from our big house to a small two-bedroom apartment in a residence hall.

We had made a choice to reach up to another level. The move to Michigan meant new opportunities. We had followed our feelings and that part of ourselves that wanted another chance, another start. I quickly realized that while we had satisfied one part of our lives, we had created anguish for ourselves and our children in moving to a racially divided city and campus.

This new world created in me a feeling of helplessness. One night, in a fit of frustration, I sat at my desk. The feeling of wanting to give up the fight completely overwhelmed me.

Looking at my sleeping children, I wrote:

> Where do you begin when you love beautiful children?
> They are beautiful (and yet not hostile to society's lack of
> change) and hopeful (despite the frustrations).
>
> I suspect and feel an anarchy within the nation, a feel-
> ing that prompts my restlessness and consumes my pas-
> sion. I want to do something, scream and say, I know, I
> know, I know. Yet I am aloof and still searching as you
> grow.
>
> You, Thomas, Jr., strong, changing, independent, alone
> yet always in company.
>
> You, Jane, strong, confused, frustrated and deciding to
> be like me but so much better. In time, you will challenge
> my style and take a giant step that will leave me breath-
> less.
>
> If I could be absorbed in you so completely, this search
> would end in some release. But I'll always be developing
> with little notion of where to go. And so I am and so will
> you be; the distance is in the racist contradictions of the
> starting point.
>
> I want to say: No more proving I am intelligent.
> Nothing can refute what I am. My weaknesses will be mis-
> interpreted, yet my strengths doggedly persist. I cannot
> tolerate cruelty and it exists. It is a bore, and I am getting
> older.
>
> You can give life in many ways: birth, helping, saving,
> feeding, clothing, praising, being and sometimes even
> dying, slowly or completely avoiding letting the notion
> finally catch you.

The risk we had taken was made painfully clear one
night. A suspicious fire broke out before Christmas on the
floor where the black women lived. That night, they had invited our daughter Jane to sleep over. I had gotten her settled
with several of the students to watch over her. After midnight,
when all was quiet, smoke stole in and quickly filled the hall.
The alarms went off, and women began to stream out of the
building. I awoke, panicked, and screamed and called for Jane.
I took Tommy outside to look for her and attend to the students

while Tom went into the building to assist the residents and find Jane. In minutes, which seemed like hours, she was led out huddled in a blanket.

I was hit square in the face with the consequences of our decision. We had to leave, and yet remain focused on our goal. In a sense, the fire at Brown Hall created new energy in us to seek out better choices. We were more conscious than ever of the importance of our journey and our responsibility to move forward.

We purchased a small house in Ann Arbor. I enrolled in a Ph.D. program at the University of Michigan and secured a position as a Teaching Fellow in the Department of Education, supervising student teachers. I felt the weight of the new culture and new demands. I felt an aloneness that most often I'd hide, yet at night I would capture my feelings in notes to myself:

> I hope that I am not too tired to write of how I feel. I'm in new company now. Two years ago I would have challenged the idle chatter, the attempts to make me feel comfortable with excerpts from their (whites') frail war games, but now I listen, tame and pleased that someone is talking to me and acknowledging my presence and assuming my intelligence. Perhaps I have always been afraid of being too close to the emotions that fire me and the people, the blacks that I know and grew to love. Perhaps that is why I left New York, home. We shared a trap, and I, because of my talk, might be expected to fight back. The danger of our dying inside was so close. I had to change something, so I changed to a different place, moved on in my search. The action perhaps of the powerless and gutless.
>
> I subjected myself to a loneliness and displacement that I didn't realize was possible and I observed and looked back in pain.
>
> We had sold the house, big and beautiful, paid a few bills that constantly seemed to haunt our living and moved to a residence hall in Yspilanti. We fantasized that the small wage and offer of a place, maintenance and furnishings would permit us the opportunity to be free of the

burdens of debt that moved with us like an albatross and promised that we would use the freedom wisely, freely, while creating no new shackles.

We soon found out, cruelly and swiftly, that our blackness could not be absorbed in our dreams. The anchor of being black existed even in the new port. We merely had given up the glorious luxury of talking it out for the maddening deep dead end of talking everything into an inner dialogue from whence there is never and can never be a response.

I have begun what I view now as participation in the ritual to affirm my existence: more education, a Ph.D. Initially hostile, I spoke with contempt as a visitor to a primitive habitat, as they tried to tame me. I later assumed their frame of reference and tried to connect, until the nonverbal responses suggested there was too little acquaintance for them to care to feel where I was or what I was trying to say.

The moving within myself has intensified. There are nights when I think my very insides will burst. I cannot tolerate drowning in the loneliness that has muted my smile, inhibited my travel and muffled my loving. Being in school is the only connection with something outside of me, and in my attempt to survive, I have acted as I was expected, acted as if I was just born and there was no life before being here, and in time, losing touch with emotions, spirits and the frame of reference of my people. If I could fly back to the fire I knew and learn to love its glow, I would do so.

That was growing up. I have spent so much needless time giving up, because for a social being it is death to be alone in this new place.

I feel at times like an exile, missing home so much that my wishing has probably made it more beautiful and complete than it ever was or could be. For the exercise with the term exile—I wonder was it self-imposed or imposed because of what I expected to happen—freedom to be can never be. I favor the thought that the exile status would exist wherever I lived—home or here, but perhaps that is just said to make me feel better.

A year into the Ph.D. program we traveled back to Lakeview to visit friends and see our old house. They viewed us as having moved on, gained ground, a perception we encouraged. But I could see from the behavior of my children that I was not alone in missing the place that had been our home. I held back tears as Jane left our friends to go outside and call the cat she'd been forced to leave when we moved. "Tiger, Tiger," she called repeatedly, appealing, from the pond close to what had been home. I held no hope that he'd appear. He had been a house cat. We had given him to neighbors but he had disappeared from their care. But Jane would not give up, and in time, Tiger appeared, scrawny, limping, now a toughened street cat. I saw too, that in holding him and saying yet another goodbye, Jane had been toughened too.

I was not happy with what I saw as the consequences of our choices. I saw my own role in making things happen as being instrumental, getting us to the next level, opening doors for us. And when the family was torn I sensed I'd failed.

The sense of failure was keen when the phone rang late one night in Ann Arbor. I answered the upstairs phone at the same time Tom picked up the downstairs phone and greeted the caller. I heard a breathless young woman blurt out, "Tom, you don't have to worry. I'm not pregnant." I was stunned and immediately distraught. In the conversation with Tom that followed, I heard but did not hear his version of how it had happened: their casual drifting together as he dealt with being alone while I focused on my doctoral studies, the initial meeting at the rink where he had taken the kids skating. I felt responsible, having caused it by somehow not tending to him as the center of our lives, not being responsive sexually after long hours in the library and not being pretty. I had, at 34, not been with any man other than Tom. Monogamy, I believed, was insured by what you contributed in a marriage, your sacrifices and your willingness to defer to your mate. I responded to his tale with the litany of what I had done, what I had given, how I had helped him as an undergraduate and graduate student, making decisions on his classes, completing his research, and making sure that he would have an education specialist degree as I obtained my Ph.D. And I spoke of our history together, and how, given our backgrounds, we had defied the odds.

I held the image of myself as a woman, a wife, walking with, yet behind, her man. I wanted the world to see him first, to be attracted to him. He was a good father. I felt the importance of his presence for them as I worked to keep our life on course by earning more credentials, more opportunities. Feeling fortunate that I had been able to attract Tom Cross, I accepted some responsibility for his indiscretion. He was honestly contrite. We agreed we would move on. Yet it wouldn't be the same. I wanted to get through the Ph.D. program quickly. Increasingly I felt it was something to do not only for us, but for me, too.

On April 12, 1971, I received a letter announcing, "Congratulations, you are now a candidate for a doctoral degree. By this formal step, the University announces to the world that you have achieved the happy stage of your doctoral studies when a group of faculty scholars as well as the offices of the Graduate School consider you fully qualified to pursue a dissertation."

I kept focusing on the choice of the word "happy" to describe this phase. "Tired" or "relieved" would have been a better choice of words. The "fully qualified" was almost amusing, because I knew firsthand that what was being presented as knowledge about urban children, single parents and problems faced by first-generation college education students was flawed. Education was a tradition in our communities. Single parents cared about their children. And first-generation college-educated students caught on quickly, because "where there is a will there is a way." Professor after professor rejected me when I questioned their assumptions. I was forever changing my doctoral advisor. I was eager to share what I had learned and to integrate my experience into what was viewed as information. I wanted my experiences to matter, to form the basis of my perspective. My advisors regarded me coldly, disdainfully. I had not read enough of their books, hadn't assimilated myself into the culture, and didn't see the advantage of being an extension of their ideas. And they hadn't heard my grandmother say so many times, throughout my early years, "Listen, take everyone's advice but use your own judgment. Make up your own mind." And I was reminded in the frequent calls from my mother, that the battles wouldn't end, "'less you stand up for yourself."

This was clear early on when one of my white male advisors encouraged me to pursue an Ed.D., a doctorate in education, and blatantly denied that a Ph.D. would give me more options. I pressed to continue in a Ph.D. program, learning from other black doctoral students that there was a pattern of not telling black students what the options meant in terms of career goals.

I knew too that once I had decided to fast-track my doctoral studies and complete the Ph.D., I had to put together a committee and get along. As luck would have it, things came together when a black female, Dr. Betty Morrison, joined the University of Michigan's education faculty. I was 34, a doctoral student, and finally experiencing my first black teacher. I didn't know what to expect but I did feel comfortable immediately. Because she was black didn't mean she was going to give us a break, as I and my fellow black students soon learned. She taught statistics and quantitative research as if they were the only courses of importance in the world, and as if we had no other courses on our schedule, let alone a life outside the university. We were told repeatedly, "The hard-nose approach is for our own good" and "This was the way I learned." We talked about her and moaned about the work, but we loved her. She trusted that we could do it and helped us understand and appreciate how we could make our point and get a serious response if we used a quantitative approach. I always felt that Betty was making it harder for me than for anyone else, yet I learned that everyone had that feeling. She guided me in the choice of research instruments, facilitated my having access to the Detroit Public Schools for my research and later, made sure that my analysis would stand the rigors of my final oral exam.

Her support of black women drew others to Michigan. Gwendolyn Baker, who was born in Ann Arbor, joined the Ph.D. program shortly after me and became a member of my research team. We had shared our aspirations and now we planned to collaborate beyond our graduate work. Another black woman joined Gwen and me a short time later. We agreed our research and future collaboration would help others behind us.

I was in touch with my dreams of being special and of making a difference. I wanted to prove myself to my family, especially the Tuckers. At the same time, I felt it necessary to downplay my achievements or how they might change things in our family. I'd make light of my Ph.D. work by saying that the degree would give me license to be eccentric or convey that I had just drifted into the program, as if on some education shopping spree. I was aware that my sister viewed our family's being in Michigan as a manifestation of "Dolores' discontent," or what she saw as my tendency to "keep pushing and driving everyone" and creating an estrangement from my family.

I was hurt and troubled by my mother's appraisal of my being in a doctoral program. It seemed to fit into what she wanted of me: to be special and to surpass the achievements of the children of her peers, as she announced so often what a good mother she had been. Yet she let me know in a many of ways that I had long ago reached what she defined as being a good daughter. Above all, I had married Tom Cross. Without using the words, she conveyed, "He was a good catch for you, my brown, sweet, but not beautiful daughter." She equated the contribution I had made in working, caring for my children and going to undergraduate school with what she had done.

But when she visited us in Ann Arbor, she waited till Tom and the kids had left on an errand before declaring, "Dolores, you'll never be happy." Her remark cut deeply. I held thoughts of how her dreams for me had set me on this quest, had driven me to achieve, to get my Ph.D. She frowned and pouted. "Don't let people into your life. Keep more to yourself. You must be careful." I tried to control the words that would set us at each other, especially words that would suggest to her that I had raised myself or the recrimination "Where were you when I needed you." Yet I hushed her with reminders of how my Aunt Jean, Uncle Sam and other family members had been there for us. She quarreled and balled her fist at me. She did not want me to feel the pain that she had of having succeeded and then reaching a threshold beyond which one cannot go. Regard and attainment can be stolen, she said, unless you guard them well. My trust and openness left me far too vulnerable, she said.

I couldn't bear her anticipating and pondering my demise. What she didn't understand and what I could not admit to her was that in growing up, I missed her embraces for the little things. I had been on a fanatic quest to please her, please the Tuckers, and gain their regard. We were on different planes in many ways, but still so connected.

She wanted me to direct my energy to her concerns. "Call my lawyer. Do what you can do to move my lawsuit along," she said, as she updated me on her discrimination case against the state of New Jersey. She wanted me to learn the lessons of her actions, while I longed to hear more about her feelings and the events that shaped her as a woman, a black woman. What I heard was who she was as a mother and what she expected of me as her daughter. I wondered, "Were we ever in touch with each other?" And I remembered. She knew me when I devoured fairy tales and believed Sleeping Beauty lived on the top of the telephone building. She knew me when I believed kissing could make you pregnant and masturbation could leave you blind. Through it all she had been there. Not to uncover the myths with facts, certainly, but she had been there, as I took one step and then another, unprepared yet willing. Her words, "Dolores, you'll never be happy," seemed less a proclamation and more a curse. She didn't realize how much stock I had set in achieving that state and how irresponsible it was of her to say that. I finally cut off the discussion by giving her a copy of my letter advising me that I was a doctoral candidate and a promise of acknowledging her in my dissertation. It would have done me no good to share with her the reality of my uncertainty, my despair in being treated as if I were an empty slate and the depth of my aloneness in this new culture.

Nor did I want to share with her that I had not learned from her how to act with courage in front of white people. I had seen and not approved of the way she tempered her words in front of white people in a manner that came off as begging. She attempted to ingratiate herself with whites, even with her lawyer. Yet she was so bold with me. And I had seen how my wise grandmother almost never said anything but "yes Ma'am" in Mrs. Sheffield's kitchen. Yet both had deep feelings, feelings at odds with those of whites. I knew as well that the severity, the seriousness, of my tone with whites related to the disrespect I had observed. In completing the Ph.D., I was in ways that I had not fully defined attempting to protect myself, ensure some independence. I couldn't, wouldn't, limit myself to being a daughter, wife, mother. I had to do more.

Passing my orals and achieving the Ph.D. didn't define competency—for my family. Being competent in our family meant much more. Are you competent in managing preadolescent children, new issues of sexual freedom, historic issues of racism and inequities in housing, education and jobs, giving back to the community? Moreover, "are you competent enough to know when to use common sense?" And "How will you manage taking care of your children, staying in touch with your family, and being true to your roots?" You were meant to figure things out, survive and contribute and manage your life with a range of other responsibilities vying for your attention. You had to focus on your goal and stay the course. You had to jump out there, oftentimes not prepared, but still you had to do it. Sometimes it hurt. I learned to value and demonstrate competencies beyond what was measured by my doctoral orals or any exam. And I knew, from my history, that while you can teach to an oral exam or any test, you can't teach to "being a strong black woman." There's so much new ground, and very often black women are the first in their generation to get a chance.

I completed my Ph.D. in August 1971, two years after leaving Lakeview and eight years after Martin Luther King Jr. delivered his "I Have a Dream" speech.

MILE 13.2

"Hey, lady, this is Boston. Pick it up," someone in the crowd shouted as I ran a sluggish 10-minute mile pace, closing in on mile 16. I didn't appreciate the comment and tried to stay focused. But I drifted into thinking of what might have been my retort: "At least I'm in it, you macho white potato" or "Lousy crowd support for Boston." The distraction from the negative thoughts began sapping my energy as I began the trudge up the course's "heartbreak hill." I brought myself back to the important task at hand: Move it, arms low, hips in, small steps, breathe, be positive. You're doing the Boston Marathon. You're running with the best of them, the elite and the back of the pack. In the end, we'll all get a finisher's medal. Just gotta keep moving, and indeed, pick it up.

By the end of the summer of 1971, we had moved more than a dozen times and lived in three states. Our children, ages 9 and 12, had been enrolled in six school districts in their school careers. That fall saw us in a plum move to Evanston, Illinois. Tom had been selected as principal of Evanston Township High School, where he would be the first black in that position. He was going in with the support of the superintendent, whom he had met at a seminar that spring. But he faced resistance from some blacks who saw him as an outsider with little chance of succeeding in a racially charged, hostile situation. And then there were whites who just didn't want the leadership of the high school to go to a black, period. In other confrontations before we had moved to Evanston, I'd been there for Tom, listening, helping and advising him on what to do. We'd work it out together and check the signs, sizing up the political climate.

But it was different in Evanston, after I had completed my work at the University of Michigan. I was making my own way at Northwestern University as assistant professor in education and director of the School of Education's master of arts in teaching program and undergraduate clinical experiences. I had to prove myself to my colleagues as they, not happily, dealt with my unconventional appointment to the graduate school.

I had learned of the friendship of the Northwestern dean of education with the University of Michigan dean of education, and shortly after our arrival in Evanston, I made an appointment with the dean. I arrived with my dissertation in hand and announced to the dean that I was looking for a job. A smile filled his face, as I, with great aplomb, described my qualifications and why he'd be doing the right thing in hiring me. I didn't know it at the time, but the approach was the right one to use with B.J. Chandler. B.J. later confided that he liked "my spunk." It matched his Missouri forthrightness.

As most new faculty do, I learned that while the dean can bend rules to hire you, your faculty peers can fire you, especially if in most issues they disagree with the dean. I was quickly made to understand how I would be judged: scholarship, teaching and service, in that order. It didn't matter that as the first black female assistant professor in the School of Education, I faced the job of developing the new undergraduate program, maintaining enrollment in the graduate program, and teaching and leading a faculty development seminar to produce an edited publication, *Teaching in a Multicultural Society*.

I felt the crush of my administrative responsibilities in building and monitoring the two teacher education programs. At the same time I realized that my credibility as a faculty member depended on my understanding and participating in the university culture. So I volunteered for university-wide committees and was elected to the faculty senate. It was my job as head of the master's program to negotiate internships for undergraduate and graduate students, assign them supervisors, and document and expand the programs.

In the long run it was easier to negotiate the internships in urban Chicago schools than it was to prepare students to succeed in these urban situations. Working with the teachers' supervisors to document incidents of cultural conflict, I was able to secure a grant from the Kellogg Foundation to support faculty coming together from Northwestern University and the University of Michigan to develop a multicultural publication. What we discussed in the faculty group was expanded in my work with doctoral students, namely, how to go about developing an area of your research interest from the perspective of your race or gender. Or to put it another way, how do you free or discover your voice and at the same time produce a dissertation that is well-researched, thoughtful and in good scholarship?

Many women and minority students had difficulty finding advisors who would work with them, an experience I knew well from being at Michigan. The handful of white women who joined the faculty during my second year at Northwestern and I all were inundated by students seeking advisors. Initially I was reluctant to join these faculty women as they scheduled meetings to talk about what we all were experiencing. It was Susan Lourenco who suggested we meet for sherry one Friday. Of the women there, Susan and I were closest in age and married with children. I didn't see her or the other women as capable of understanding racism and how my experience differed from theirs.

I strode into the meeting with my very full Afro and a frown on my face. How could I as a black, benefit from this meeting? I asked. The conversation began, and I stayed and listened to the similarities—and differences—of our experiences. None of the three women had completed her dissertation, and yet each was an assistant professor. I was observing their privilege as white women. I called their attention to the difference in our assignments. As assistant professors they were not involved in directing major programs. Yet I had the responsibility of scholarship, teaching and service as well as running the master of arts in teaching program and the undergraduate clinical program for teachers. As I spoke, however, I realized as well that this group of women was the only group who had reached out to me in my time at Northwestern. We were, to a person, concerned about our futures at

Northwestern. We felt it was likely we were stationed near a revolving door. We continued to meet. No one at that time was committed to the success of this contigent of women. I was later to find that none of the women in our group was offered retention or promotion opportunities.

While I was involved and strong, I was aware of how my assignment at Northwestern challenged my relationship with Tom. I simply was not there to help him as I had in the past. No longer did we talk out his experiences and trials, which were considerable in his Evanston principalship. A core group of white faculty had begun to pick at his administration; the blacks stood back waiting for him to reach out to them. His support from the superintendent was not enough.

When it became clear that things were not going well for Tom at Evanston Township High, I felt responsible, confused. And while I realized that racism was playing its part in cutting short his tenure, I knew as well that we were unrealistic in expecting so much change, wanting so much change, based on how our lives had accelerated. Both of us were torn between when to express our anger and when it was best not to. Should we be passive or militant? I wanted Tom to fight back, to mimic what I saw in black militant behavior. I wanted him not to expect me to be out there with my anger, but to boldly challenge what was going on. Get mad when you're demeaned! Challenge the blacks who continue to spurn you as an outsider! I wanted to shout sometimes.

He brooded, retreated and became distracted in his love of cars, his flying lessons. He retreated to areas of comfort by retelling his exploits on the basketball court or his travels in Spanish-speaking countries. When I got phone calls from students or colleagues, he left the room so he didn't have to hear me, the intimate and helpful tone in my voice.

Until that point in our lives, I had lived with Tom as I had seen other black women live with their men. They existed not for themselves, but for their men. Yet I had begun trying to do both—live for myself and live for him. When our relationship was crumbling, I was most often asked, "What are you doing to Tom?" One Saturday, I cried and cried, slumping into a depression that lasted for days and required treatment. Tom never understood my frustration in knowing that my support of him had not empowered him enough to protect himself, his family.

I could not imagine a future that did not include Tom, yet I knew our relationship was taking a different shape as I anticipated the end of his appointment as principal of Evanston Township. I did not foresee an easy road to tenure and promotion at Northwestern University. It was time to move on again, time for me to take the lead as we looked for the next opportunity.

A move would mean disrupting Tommy and Jane at a difficult point for them. They were beginning to experience close friendships, much like what they had felt in Lakeview. Jane shared sleepovers and her deepest thoughts with her friend Carol. Tommy had attended Northwestern's music camp and was looking forward to attending Evanston Township High School.

But Claremont Graduate School in California beckoned. Tommy and Jane listened to me on the phone as I negotiated our move to California so I could become associate professor and director of teacher education. "Mom's job" was behind this move, and from this they concluded that I'd been behind all the moves they had made in their lives. I saw their hurt, yet what mattered most was what the change could mean for Tom. I saw it as an opportunity to not only begin again, but for Tom to have access to yet another opportunity. Indeed, he secured a teaching position as an adjunct professor at LaVerne College and enrolled briefly in LaVerne's Law School. We told ourselves and our families that we were moving on with our successes, intent on new achievements.

Yet with this move, I knew I'd be moving to be more alone. I anticipated a time of reckoning when I would need a circle of friends and there would be no one. I missed the support system that living in one place provides. I had had support in New York. And for a time I felt that the uniqueness that

Lakeview provided could be found in other places. It just was not so. I kept new friends at a distance while looking back to the family and friends in whose company wild ideas could be shared, truths explored and insecurities bared. Getting too close, becoming too familiar where there was mere acquaintanceship could make you vulnerable.

Our first stop that summer of 1974 was to visit my Aunt Jean and Uncle Sam. My uncle's health was beginning to fail. He was not yet 60, yet he had had two operations and wore a bag that had to be changed. He hadn't stopped working, but he had moved his office to my Aunt Jean's kitchen to spread his insurance accounts across the table and be in her company. He did not talk about his physical problems, but wanted to hear of our successes and how any of what we were doing helped black people. We heard again of the alliances he had made with Italian politicians and his concerns about some of the young Negro politicians who, to his thinking, just didn't listen. And he spoke about the New Newarkers' lack of respect for property. He alluded to his concerns for Aunt Jean's future and mistakes he may have made in being so generous to other people. There was a sadness in his voice as he said he wished he'd done more for her.

Aunt Jean cautioned him not to get excited, as she removed the paper from the dishes and utensils she used to protect them from the roaches that came when she accepted my sister Jean and me and all our roach-filled things into her home so many years before. We sat down to eat and I noticed Aunt Jean's nod of approval at my hair. For the visit, I had pressed out my Afro, and I was wearing traditional clothing. They did not ask me about Northwestern or what happened to Tom at Evanston. They didn't expect California to be easy. In response to our move to Claremont, I heard from my uncle what I had heard with every move we had made: "Dolores, what difference is all this going to mean to our people? How will you give back to the community?" I tried to link it all together as I told him of preparing future leaders. And I tried briefly to win his praise by mentioning the book I was editing.

I felt him saying I had not done enough and I hadn't yet pleased him. I longed for his praise and to hear him say, "You're just like a Tucker." It didn't happen. When he got to asking about my church-going, I took an opportunity to assert and differ with him by arguing that the church had done little to rectify the problems of black people. To which he responded: "You sound like your father, Charlie." I noticed he could not say, "My brother, Charlie."

Our time in New Jersey included a visit with my sister and her family. She missed us, asking, "Why are you moving so far from family?" Regarding all of our trials as stressful, Jean told us we should relax and have fun. "Dolores, lighten up!" I raised questions about the books her children were reading and the quality of their school work. I wanted to impress upon her that it was tough out there; you had to be good to make it. At one point I brought her children, Steven and Karen, into what my children called "Mom's philosophical discussions," and I asked: "What are your aspirations?" "How do you expect to achieve them?" and "Tell me what do you know about current events?" I was expecting my children to set an example in their responses and to raise the bar for my sister's children. What my niece and nephew heard was me saying, "You're not special."

My sister broke the tension with the suggestion of a game. But I was intent on their learning from my experience, appreciating me as a resource and viewing what I was doing as paving the way for them. I realized too that I had to make my point without conveying how much we had been bruised in trying to succeed. That would only discourage them. And besides, I knew they felt that my ambitions created a problem. They preferred hearing about successes through newsclips. For them, I would have made it when my picture was in *Jet* or *Ebony*. My sister wanted me to tell and live an uncomplicated story.

I wanted my family to know some of the values I brought to higher education—what kept me going. I had then—and still have—a strong conviction that access to higher education is facilitated by information. There must be a support system. Legislation must encourage universities to promote access. Blacks have a rich legacy of producing achievers and a strong tradition that values education. I wanted to be an example, be someone others could learn from. I went into higher education knowing that no matter what the job was, my life's work was to facilitate access, to convey my strong convictions and to remember who I was. I went into higher education feeling as I did in my marriage that my role was to be instrumental, not to be necessarily the star.

I wrote in my diary:

> In every move—from New Jersey to New York to Michigan to Illinois and now to California—I find myself asking, "Will it do that there are more flowers, trees, soft grass and flowering bushes? Can I absorb it all and somehow in new places grow away from the culture, voices and values that nursed me? And if I do, who will I be?" And why, as I hold on to the reminders of my starting point, home, do I have moments of displeasure that my mother is my mother? I am aware of a dilemma. I recall with each previous phase, while I am overcoming new hurdles, feeling annoyed when someone would remark that I looked or acted like my mother. It would make me uncomfortable, as the saying meant that perhaps like her, I would not be taken seriously. Like her my lips would always appear as pouting. Like her I'd be viewed as odd. And like her, I would be viewed as a child. I didn't want to look like her, and I didn't want to inherit the centuries of constraints and stereotypes perceived by others in my mother. And now, smoothing some of the wrinkled spaces of the past, I acknowledge with pride: my mother is my blackness.
>
> While in Claremont there will be more flowers, trees, mountains, attractive bushes and warm weather, there will be evenings when the only phone call will be from my mother. She will call as if she is next door rather than from the projects in Newark. And I will listen carefully to what she is saying and how she is sorting the "why" of my behavior from what she has to say. I hear that my credentials keep her bragging. She knows the game of professor

doesn't pay much but she is proud. "Dolores, please send me clippings,"she says, "How do you feel, and are you eating all right? I know you are tired. I hope you are not going out too much, and please don't let people use you." She continues, "How are the kids? Are they home? They run too much. Are their shoes too tight? Have you checked? Does Jane need underwear? I really miss my babies." And despite the distance, "Dolores, I am glad you're there. The family would just wear you out. You really don't need anyone. It's pretty out there. Are you sure you are resting? Dolores you must take care of your health. I worry about you, and what would I do if something happened to you?" I talked to my friends. Their kids are fine, but not doing as well as you, Dolores. I won't tell them where you are because they will want to visit and pester you, and you're too busy.

I will hear her courting me if I should mention favorably someone she sees as her peer. 'Dolores, you don't owe them anything. I went to night school for almost 20 years. I take exams and have my lawyer dealing with my civil service assignment. I am going to Trenton to follow up on my rights.' She will tell me how much she enjoyed the long bus trips to visit me in Michigan and Illinois. Now she'll have a trip to California. Should she feel I fail to appreciate her, she'll assert, "I am your mother."

At times, when her bills begin to bother her and her job becomes a hassle, her voice whines, soft and secretive, as if someone else is listening. It's at these times when she demands, admonishes, "You would be able to help me, if your habits weren't so foolish. Stop visiting, save your money and remember I am getting older." I hear her saying that perhaps she'll be displaced from her apartment as she was years ago. As she talks, I visualize her apartment. It's cluttered, yet there's a feeling that something is taking shape. Sewing patterns for clothes for herself and her grandchildren are in various stages of completion. Old souvenirs from trips are displayed. Ticket stubs, clippings, letters to lawyers and politicians and her club members are on her desk. And I know despite the disarray it all has meaning. There is evidence in the contents of her place of her dealing with her gender, race, age, and status—and it's cluttered. She does not know the depth of or difference in my listening and my beginning to solve the dilemma, the contradictions within me.

I am seeing that my mother had once been a child, a young adult, with questions and dreams, and like me, has had to cope with the time and circumstance of her entry into history. I have a better understanding of her linking of herself to me. My mother is my blackness, and in saying I know this reality, I will never be seduced to forget who I am. I won't be taken in by the flowers, mountains, soft grass and bushes of Claremont's Never-Never land.

It feels good to be past the point of acting as if I was immaculately conceived. I don't expect that kissing can transform a frog into a prince or that embracing can transform ugly into lovely. Nor do I expect to live happily ever after. I want to relate to realities in ways that change me.

MILE 14

The road surface feels a little strange, but I know I'll get used to it. The impact forces on roads aren't that different from the forces on trails. These new surfaces will strengthen my tendons and ligaments. I'm away from sights and sounds that distract me. I have to be careful not to run too fast until I get to know the course. I have to remember to watch my footing. The road looks pretty, but it's deceptive. I don't want to sprain an ankle before I really get going.

You learn that while there are new opportunities, you're bound by the sociopolitical times. While I and others like me had changed and gained new experiences and were prepared to join the ranks of our white peers at the next level, the trials of one place would by and large happen in the next. Access was a first step, the tease. You're accepted in the door, weighed down with responsibilities and expected to be superwoman. There could be no excuses. You're in it not only for your own self-respect and in honor of those who went before you, but for food, clothing and shelter.

The first African American woman to hold a faculty rank at the Claremont Graduate School, I had been hired as an associate professor and director of teacher education. While I had taught at Northwestern and gained high marks from students for my teaching and advising, I knew there was no possibility of my being retained, let alone being recommended for tenure, if I failed to implement new state guidelines, grow the program and meet the faculty criteria for scholarship, teaching and service. I had to wear four hats well. I was clearly in peril.

Tenure was an issue from the start. It was through networking at meetings of the American Educational Research Association that I found other African American faculty members who faced challenges similar to mine. We were, for the most part, the only people of color on the faculty of research universities. As we were adjusting to the culture, we were being sought out as African American faculty members by students and drawn to service commitments.

I found myself talking on an almost daily basis to James Deslonde, an African American assistant professor at Stanford University. We talked of the pressure and demands of getting published and being there for students. We shared what we picked up from professional groups, mentored each other as black peers and agreed to collaborate in writing articles.

It was Jim who urged me to stay the course as senior editor for the book *Teaching in a Multicultural Society,* which looked at the impact of multicultural education on teachers in training. Jim contributed a chapter. Gwendolyn Baker, Ph.D., joined me as an editor. Gwen had been instrumental in my previous research as I gathered data for my dissertation. As black women, Gwen and I shared the struggle of juggling family and academic responsibilities as we completed our Ph.Ds at Michigan. Given my responsiblities as an administrator, it was essential to colloborate with peers, edit publications and develop chapters and articles to meet the requirements for publishing.

As at Northwestern, students at Claremont experienced me as an African American aware of the complexities of advancing a point of view from one's cultural perspective and someone clear about the reality of racism. They also experienced me as a woman willing to nurture, cultivate interests and lend my feminine voice to a discussion of issues.

I used the same process I used in putting together *Teaching in a Multicultural Society* to get students to critique points of view in a multicultural society. Students consulted with experts and worked in small groups and teams to critique their approaches to their disciplines. Were they inclusive? Did stereotypes prevail? Was the research honest? I presented for their discussion typical incidents from elementary and secondary schools that revealed various kinds of responses by teachers to the cultural differences of students. Open comparisons of the perceptions, attitudes, alternative idea and experiences of members of the teams also proved worthwhile.

In the fall of 1975, a diverse group of concerned and energetic doctoral students joined me in my class. They were there to study multicultural education. Some came to the class out of curiosity, others came with a burning desire to learn creative ways of fostering social change. They were mostly working educators, involved as teachers, administrators and researchers. As a group they reflected different cultures, races and linguistic backgrounds as well as various preferences and perspectives. Each had observed in varying degrees the impact of the civil rights movement and the increased attentiveness to human rights in the United States. As a group they brought the force of having experienced life from different cultural perspectives that would stimulate an important inquiry of multicultural education.

A basic premise of multicultural education is that the differences that characterize individuals and groups should be cherished and cultivated for the benefits they bring to all people. An honest intellectual response to multicultural reality requires each person to face his or her own social environment boldly and accept personal responsibility for being a productive member. As such, I invited my students to perceive multicultural awareness as fundamentally a moral question. They were participating in processes that extended levels of morality and developed for them the moral authority to learn and teach in ways that recognized and cherished individual differences. This meant consciously assessing, critiquing and reviewing personal as well as research directions to ensure fairness and a respect for diversity. I expected the students to be at different places in their understanding of the issues and experience with the process. I also expected them to support and help each other and provided team or triad work to facilitate small group discussion.

The essential questions were: What is the effect of new information upon the self and one's perception of one's role? How does the individual make new information meaningful? In what way is moral thinking or moral authority involved? What is the end result? A commitment to openness and a will-

ingness to explore and take risks were required. I used myself
as an example, looking at the influence on my perspective of
this starting point as an African American woman with urban
roots. So much has been written about urban blacks that does
not reflect the competencies developed and the ability of urban
people to champion over adversity. An acknowledgment of
that reality should affect the scholar and educator. Yet there is
paucity of literature that speaks to the strengths of the urban
poor, which creates a situation where there are low expectations. Education was a tradition in my family and community, a tradition that should be recognized and indeed saluted
given the constraints of the day.

I continued the practice of requiring the doctoral students
to write papers on their reactions to my lectures, our discussions and class projects. I used the information to shape my
lectures and add to what I knew of my teaching. The interaction over time among supportive, caring professional peers
greatly aided their individual growth toward moral autonomy
on significant issues. I asked the students to develop a viable
perspective that reflected the integrity of diversity. They were
encouraged as well to examine issues of fairness in ensuring
that all groups were given a chance. I wanted the course to
help them seek a dissertation topic with authority and take the
risk of developing a perspective that recognized and celebrated their cultural contributions as well as the integrity of other
cultures.

In the end, I wanted these doctoral students to appreciate
the power of learning, to experience its enormous enabling
potential and understand that it is not simply an abstraction
relegated to the four walls of a classroom. Most of all I wanted them to understand that learning cannot be achieved simply by collecting information. For understanding to occur,
information must have meaning. Meaning in turn requires
understanding.

My advisor responsibilities, publishing pressures and
administrative responsibilities were made easier by my enjoy-
ment of teaching. In the classroom I could promote growth by

accepting the validity of points of view emanating from a cultural perspective like or different from my own.

As an example, Margo Long, a white female, challenged the myths about miscegenation, specifically, the mixture of black and white. Based upon an extensive review and rethinking of social science evidence, she presented a systematic refutation of prevailing assumptions. Another student, Barbara Richardson, a black female, presented information about the historical development and current structure of black families that brought into serious question traditional thinking about black families, namely, that they are "culturally deprived," "at a deficit" and "pathological."

Rosa Casarez, a Hispanic female, taught me how my words of encouragement could help someone whose background was different from my own. Rosa was quiet during classes, yet there was passion in her writing. I invited her to make an appointment with me. In that meeting, I urged her to pursue a Ph.D. and communicate with others with her very powerful voice. She was transformed before me. She was animated. I knew she was on her way to big things.

At the end of the day, after a late class, I would return home, humming and singing and turn to my records and sing with Aretha, Ray Charles, O.C. Smith and Nina. Tom and the kids knew when I was returning from teaching. They also knew that in the classroom I felt support for my ideas and a validation of my presence as a black female with a perspective.

My passion had an impact on my family, as members of my class became extended family. I became involved in their lives, coaching and being available as a friend.

At the same time, I was not always there to share Jane's success in track and field events and Tommy's success in the marching band. I felt that my role in helping others to stretch and find their voices helped Jane and Tommy. I would speak to them of what I had to do as a warrior involved in a revolution, making a difference. The ideals I sought to project for my children were those of the economically independent working mother and a black woman unsheltered by the times. There

was no other way, given how far I had come. I could not quit.
Somehow I had to do it all and keep on going. I felt in touch
with the starting point of my culture, yet affected by all that
had happened since I left Newark. I believed that I was making a statement that would endure as deeply as the statements
of my ancestors, Harriet Tubman and Sojourner Truth. I'd seen
in women who went before me determination that was founded on unwavering faith in their ability to make a difference.

I wanted as well to be judged for my message, vision and
contribution. I sought to model what a commitment to diversity meant when one was an administrator. Over the course of
a year I worked with faculty at San Diego State University to
forge an agreement for a joint doctoral program with a multicultural focus between Claremont Graduate School and San
Diego State University. The program meant that students
enrolled at Claremont had a more diverse faculty community
to work with and that the diverse student body at San Diego
State University had access to doctoral study at Claremont
Graduate School. It was the first joint doctoral program
between a public and private university in the state of
California. The program continued for many years after my
tenure at the Graduate School.

At Claremont I took risks and raised questions. In faculty meetings I brought up concerns expressed by students about
how fairly scholarship that challenged prevailing views was
judged. Some faculty who perceived themselves as being
without bias thought the issue was my own personal problem.
I was aware of their making judgments about others based on
their color or language. On one occasion, I overheard male faculty members talking about how they had been distracted by
the size of a female student's breasts to the point where they
hadn't heard a word she was saying. Students who easily won
faculty support were those for whom diversity never was an
issue or those willing to work on a professor's research issue,
rather than taking a risk to develop their own point of view.
Diversity was often treated in a negative context, such as when
less rigorous programs were crafted for a culturally diverse

group of Los Angeles school administrators. These programs, to my thinking, tracked them in much the same way as the Ed.D. tended to track doctoral candidates to positions outside research universities. The few opportunities for doctoral study for women and minorities were largely in the social sciences.

Yet with all its problems, Claremont Graduate School's Department of Education enrolled graduate students from diverse backgrounds. The greatest challenge of the times for Claremont as well as all educational institutions was to understand diversity for what it is: an enriching, valuable asset that should not be squandered.

I was fortunate to find in Peter Drucker a friend and colleague who communicated respect for me as someone who was not content to play in the shallows. He told me he admired my propensity to go into deep waters, where the winds and currents can be tricky, even dangerous. I felt from Peter a genuine interest in my success and confidence in my ability to add value to any situation. He appreciated that I had worked to develop a perspective, a style that was influenced but not controlled by my blackness. He and his wife, Doris, did not stand in the distance. They were not afraid to join me and become involved with my family.

Peter and Doris had seen Ntozake Shange's play, *for colored girls who have considered suicide/when the rainbow is enuf*. Peter sensed a stiffness, a lack of flow in the movement of the women. In his view, there was none of the sensuous sway and gentleness evident in movies and plays depicting black women in the 1940s and 1950s. I focused on the dialogue of the women and how they seemed to have given up on black men. Living in Claremont, I felt I was missing this kind of dialogue. And it was difficult to put my finger on the change that was occurring between black men and black women. It seemed that black men and black women in the 1950s and 1960s were in tune, yet caught up in dealing with a larger political, social and economic challenges. My impressions and expectations of black men and black women friends in the 1970s arose from the joys, struggles and hopes of these times. We were young blacks in the struggle. But now, to my thinking, we were very different because of our independence and the different challenges we faced.

MILE 15

Stay focused. Look ahead at what you are prepared to do. You've established a base, found your center. Let confidence kick in when uncertainty appears like a cloud. Slow down if you need to, but maintain your form: arms low, heel-toe, hips tucked in. Listen for your breath. Move out carefully but with assurance as you do your best.

I received the call I'd been dreading. Uncle Sam's condition had worsened. My Aunt Jean called to let me know that he was in the hospital. She had cared for him at home as long as she could. She didn't have to ask me to come. Jane and I left on the next plane. Arriving in Newark, I saw that in the almost ten years since the riots, little had happened to restore the city. Life had not gotten better for the elders in my family. I was shocked to see Uncle Sam bedridden, stilled, with gangrene-covered legs and diabetes. He had rejected having his legs amputated and had resigned himself to dying. Aunt Jean read to him, holding his hand. She was with him all day and night. Dark circles ringed her eyes. Her strength of character, cleanness of soul and unselfish spirit filled the room.

I realized in watching them how much they'd endured from his first work experience as a Pullman porter and hers as a maid and nanny. I marveled at the dignity of their lives and the moment. Jane sat in the corner of the hospital room and intently began writing in her journal. She seemed so much older than 13, and I felt her absorption and concern for me as well as for her great uncle.

Watching Uncle Sam, I regretted that he had not seen more change in the city he loved and for the people he loved. Would it be the same for me? Worse yet, would it be the same for my children? Would they make the transition from life to death disheartened by the lack of caring for the poor and disadvantaged? Uncle Sam was glad that Jane and I had come from California. I expected him, as he'd done so often, to interview me on the depth of my contribution and the impact I was having on the community. Instead he spoke of what mattered most to him, Aunt Jean. He apologized for leaving without preparing her. While he had done well in his insurance business, he had not planned to die first and imagined he'd be there always to protect Aunt Jean. He asked me to look out for her and not to forget her. I promised and committed myself to being her caregiver.

My aunt had, like many black women of her generation, planned how she would make do if her husband should die first. She owned what had been her parents' home in Belleville, New Jersey, and viewed her elegant French furniture as her insurance plan.

My uncle died shortly after my visit in the spring of 1975. I learned from Aunt Jean what would be my pattern of support. I'd visit periodically and do her shopping, thread needles of every color, get money orders for her bills and donations to Billy Graham and her church, and do her correspondence and Christmas cards six months in advance. And I respected her preference for being alone with her *Bible*, books, photos, and closets and drawers of Uncle Sam's clothing.

I helped her move out of the apartment she'd shared with my uncle for over 30 years and into a senior citizens' building. I never once heard her speak a critical word of my uncle and what he'd not tended to. I believe she saw her life as better than most. Her view did not reflect the advantages of some white women her age. To her thinking, white women were not caught in the struggle; their husbands did not bear the burden my uncle had assumed. Yet, she had created a world of beautiful color and elegance in her apartment and was flawlessly dressed when she went shopping or to church, proud that her taste was better than that of most white women. Aunt Jean and Uncle Sam valued and were driven by the notion of contribution, believing in God and living a principled life to make a difference. I saw theirs as the perfect marriage.

I admired how Aunt Jean had been instrumental to Uncle Sam and wondered if it would have been different if they had had children. Could she have made the same sacrifices, given in the ways parents must support children? I knew the answer was yes.

Tom Jr.'s high school graduation was several months away. He was 18, and I was yet to be 40. We laughed at the thought that he'd be going to college, just as I was paying off my student loan. It didn't seem possible, but there it was. I was struck by the reality that in our growing up as parents his future was no better planned than his birth. He was looking into colleges as I was realizing, "There's so much I want to tell you to prepare and inspire you." He had joined us in civil rights demonstrations and seen me stressed out by racism. And he observed how I filled my days with matters of consequence, going on and on about injustices of our day.

He and Jane were encouraged to be independent, shop for themselves and prepare their own meals. They each had a car and were supported in their love of sports, music and theatre. Most important, they were liberal in their views

Yet, through all of my experiences, who had I become? This question was posed to me by an old friend from Newark, Mary Hazel, while visiting us in Claremont the year before my 40th birthday. In her streetwise and rapid-fire manner, Mary shared in expletives the world as she saw it and as she thought I should see it. I loved the rhythm of her voice amidst the monotone of Claremont.

Mary went on about the accomplishments and frailties of my children, her children, Tom, Sr., and more. She was clear in her admiration for my mother, who encouraged her to be successful and get an education. "Your mother always has something good to say. She gets around. She loves you, Dolores," said Mary. She continued with a spirit of compassion and concern:

Honor your mother, Dolores. Are you still trying to do everything? When are you going to learn to delegate? You can't do everything. They'll be the first to praise you and use you. You're too good, Dee. These niggers will use you, and the white man will use you up and keep on stepping. Nothing has changed. The whites still hate you. The more you get, the worse it is. And you're out here by yourself.

Equality's not there, Dee. Charlie [the white man] is still out here screwing us all. But I gotta give it to you. You got out of the projects, put that lanky drink of water Tom, through school, put yourself through, got a Ph.D. Now you're here away from the crap but still working hard. Dee, you're looking good, keeping the weight down, doing okay, but how's Dee really?

Mary went on, but all I heard was, like a siren in my head, "How's Dee really?" She was searching casually for the essence behind the mask of titles and credentials and my diatribes about matters of consequence.

That spring before Tom Jr. graduated, I collected my diary entries from age 13, journal notes and letters to family and friends and created the document "How's Dee Really," a chronicle of events that included him and the rest of the family and my feelings about the events of our lives. He knew me as his mother, a spouse and an educator. Through the document I communicated my feelings, the feelings of a black woman. I don't know how I found the time to create the book, but I was driven by a sense of urgency to prepare him and the feeling that I'd not given enough of myself to him.

In my dreams, he continued to be a young boy, yet he was a young man, and I had not prepared him for all that it meant. During his growing-up years, I minimized, as I feel some black women do, the importance of making sure our boys feel a part of our lives. Tommy didn't experience my work world, and there were too few times when just Tommy and I were together.

At the same time, I encouraged a larger-than-life relationship with his father. My husband was a good father, willing to involve Tom Jr. in his interests. As a son, Tom Jr. must have been proud to have such a tall father, a former basketball player and fluent Spanish speaker. I felt there was less to show off as it related to me. I was slim and attractive by some standards, yet prone to get into a debate or display my impatience at anything that appeared in the slightest way racist. I was proud of how Tom Jr. had discovered in music a means to finding a community. His sense of humor, willingness to improvise in any situation and propensity to take the lead helped him make friends.

Since leaving Lakeview, we had lived in predominantly white communities. Claremont was the whitest. I worried whether Tom Jr. was prepared as a black man to deal with the racism he'd find without the support of his family. I didn't want him to expect too much. Moreover, I wanted him to realize that while I'd been out there trying to make a difference, I had changed, but nothing much else had changed. In "How's Dee Really," I wrote the following:

> I didn't expect as a child or teen and even a decade ago that the circumstances in the space I occupy would not have changed as I enter my 40s.
>
> Hadn't we nonviolently dealt with spitting, pushing, senseless killing?
>
> Hadn't we articulated the right phrases, reviewed the literature and impressed you?
>
> Hadn't we said, "We hurt?"
>
> Hadn't we sacrificed our children, friends and family and been at times without support systems to be involved in the cause and sing "We Shall Overcome?"
>
> And hadn't we passed those objective tests and altered fond traditions, like having fun on Saturday nights, and kept our families intact?
>
> Hadn't we gone to work suppressing our hostility and come home drained?
>
> Then, we should have expected greater changes and not be regarded, each credentialed black soul, as an exception. It should be understood that there are more like me in Newark and every damned urban ghetto. Some reports

on conflicts today seem like reruns of old movies. The losers are the same: people of color, with the difference being that the movement's liberals are casualties, too. Folks are back wanting peace and quiet, and saying they can't stand ghetto language, can't stand angered blacks, can't stand their demands. And they politely request that you don't deal with issues through the starting point of your culture, in my case, black. The changes we expected were naively pursued given the reality of racism. There hasn't been enough time to deal with its fury. My eyes smart when I'm alone. Is it a question of time? Of sheer will?

I am a black woman, not a saint. I hurt, and sometimes late at night I rock my pillow, missing my children as babies. No mother can love more dearly than a black mother and none is more dearly loved.

I am doing the best I can to make an impression on my family and friends, and yes, to make an impression on foes who sometimes berate me and make light of the strength of strong black women and men who preceded me and those who will follow.

I find myself mumbling, "Du Bois was enlightened and died in exile." And others experience without madness what I mean in saying, "So much remains the same, but I've changed."

Ozie Olean Johnson Tucker
mother

Charlie Tucker, father

JeanTucker, aunt

SamTucker, uncle

(Seated) James Tucker, the Rev. Thomas T. Tucker, Roger
Tucker (Standing) Franklin Tucker, Samuel Tucker,
Matthew Tucker

Dolores, age 12

Dolores, age 16

Jean, age 9 and Dolores
Tucker, age 8

Claremont CA, 1970s

Jane Cross,
daughter, age 4

Tom Cross Jr.
son, age 8

With Tom Cross Sr.

Jane, age 16

Tom Jr. in 1976

With Tom Jr.

Jane

Jean McRae and family
Tina, Karen,
Jean, Jake and Steven

Tom Jr., Ozie Tucker, Jane

At age 50, New York City Marathon
4 hours, 42 minutes

Chicago Marathon
3 hours, 57 minutes,
1992

Twin Cities Marathon
3 hours, 37 minutes,
1998

Inauguration as
President at CSU,
1991

Chicago State University
president's mansion

Running with CSU students, 1994

CSU student center and
residence hall built during
Cross Administration, 1995

Groundbreaking
ceremony with Illinois
Gov. Jim Edgar and
Chicago Mayor Richard
Daley

With Haki R. Madhubuti and Alice Walker,
CSU Black Writer's Conference, 1995

With Gwendolyn Brooks,
Poet Laureate of Illinois

With Nelson Mandela,
South Africa, 1996

James Willis

With Jacoby Dickens, Chair of
Seaway Bank and CSU Board of
Trustees

MILE 16

Remember, pain is the body's way of telling you that something is wrong. You can't maintain a hard training program if you're experiencing pain.

By 1978, my husband and I had been married for 22 years and we were in denial. We were movng apart. I'd amuse our friends by the way I sang Tom's name. I'd be equally amused as they said "Tom and Dee" as if it were one name. Our professional lives dominated our communications with friends and family. They didn't realize how separate our lives had become. I was deep into my challenge as the lone black female at the graduate school, and Tom was struggling as the first black principal at Ontario Junior High School in Ontario, California, his adjunct faculty appointment not having worked out.

Staying afloat financially while we acquired and maintained things provided the focal point of our most serious conversations. We had been educated and credentialed, yet we were still struggling. Tom felt we'd do better financially if we sold Amway products. He added up what we both might make in our respective careers as a college faculty member and a school administrator and suggested more lucrative careers as Amway representatives. It was difficult at first for me to realize he was serious. But I knew as he discussed it that he was under some pressure at his job. He saw this new direction as a means to an end. It seemed to me that we couldn't abandon our professional dreams and our responsibility as educators. We'd come too far. The suggestion of going into sales mocked my commitment and passion. He did the arithmetic about how much time it took to make $18,000 a year as a faculty member, to which I'd say it wasn't about money. I refused to help him make this happen. We talked about counseling, but we didn't follow through. We chose instead to deny the pain and the weakening of the bond between us.

Our living separate lives became apparent to me one morning when I noticed that some of Tom's clothes were not in his closet. The meaning hit me like a sledgehammer. We'd both been flirting. But this was different. This hurt. I didn't want our marriage to end.

I remembered that he said he'd be playing tennis that morning. I gathered up the items remaining in his closet, dumped them in the trunk and went out to look for him. I felt a panic, loss, sorrow and anger as I drove around. In time I found him playing tennis with a young redheaded woman who had been at one of his Amway parties. I emptied the contents of my car on the tennis court and returned home, where I waited for hours until he returned.

The woman was a single parent of two children in his school. She shared his interest in sales. It was "something that happened." I felt immediately that I'd been careless. I couldn't imagine a life without him. We had failed each other. Not being able to "hold on to" Tom Cross, I thought at the time, would negate all my successes.

MILE 16.4

A runner is able to transcend and redefine traditional standards of beauty. A beautiful face may include pronounced cheek bones, clear eyes and ruddy skin that glows from exertion. A beautiful body may be defined by its upper and lower body strength and how that strength can enhance the runner's ability to progress from start to finish.

Most beautiful is a runner—flushed, sweaty, somewhat disheveled, totally uncaring about how she looks—crossing the finish line, victorious in her knowledge that she went the distance.

At 40, I became aware that I had to redefine myself and accept and embrace what it would take to ensure an economic independence that would permit me to make a contribution and at the same time have money in my checking account. Increasingly, I'd remember Aunt Jean's words to me: "Your children did not ask to be born." These words reminded me of my responsibility. I had persevered and been true to the traditions of the strong black women before me in being instrumental to my man. And I had let my work take me in the direction of uplifting my race. But at 40, I had to transcend that definition of the beautiful life and do what was necessary to make sure that my children had a chance. And I had to take some risks to keep my marriage and stay whole.

I took direction from the mirror, appreciating the eyes that met me (like my mother's eyes) and the soft brown skin that framed me (like my father's skin). Viewing my head, face and body as one does a sculpture, I proceeded to have my teeth capped, my hair permed into a softer Afro and lose 12 pounds.

All the time I was preparing myself for an undefined transition, moving from being instrumental to taking the lead, and doing so unashamedly. I was making this transition aware of the support my children would need to get an education and aware of how it might affect my relationship with my husband at a critical point in his life.

At stake was our 22 years of marriage, our special way of supporting each other without interfering in matters of education and career, and that part of our lives that we had shared with each other. Tom was anticipating his resignation as principal at Ontario Junior High School and looking to improving his finances through sales.

When the opportunity came in spring 1978 for me to pursue the position of vice chancellor of student affairs and special programs at the City University of New York, we did not, as a family, discuss the depth of the disruption the job would mean or the turning point it would be in our relating to each other. We had to stabilize our finances. To me that meant moving ahead while at the same time making a contribution consistent with my values. Tom Jr. was in his second year as a music major at Sonoma State University. And at 16, Jane would be graduating that summer and traveling on an American Field Service (AFS) program to Mombasa, Kenya, after which she would be attending the University of California at Davis.

I had envisioned a life filled with teaching, empowering future scholars and educators, and reading and writing to build on what I was learning about helping students, especially minorities and women, find their own voice. I'd wanted to live in a place like Claremont, an oasis of trees, small shops and beautiful flowers, and from such a place maintain my urban connection and give back as a teacher and scholar. Those were bold dreams for a black woman.

But in the job at the City University of New York, I saw a means to help my family, teach through what I did as an administrator and transcend the traditional role of a black woman caregiver. I knew as well that it might mean my moving ahead alone. The response I got from Betty Morrison, my advisor at Michigan, was similar to what I'd hear from friends and members of my family. "You need Tom. You need his presence. You can't be out there as a woman alone. It is just too tough." Similar sentiments were voiced by my sister when she reminded me that we had been "Dolores and Tom" for over

20 years. They didn't say it outright, but I heard: "Your attractiveness is related, bound, to his head-turning presence."

In my eyes, I was prepared to enter the new arena, take the risk alone. In accepting the position in New York I was saying, "I'll show them" to skeptics as well as to some colleagues at Claremont Graduate School who did not see my full value as I came up for tenure.

James Deslonde also had been denied tenure at Stanford. In a conversation with him I heard the depth of his devastation as he considered the impact that the denial would have on his family. We spent time communicating about the wins and losses in the struggle as we recalled changes in our personal lives since *Brown v. Board*. We focused on how all we had done had affected our relationship with our spouses and children. He also talked about missing time with his mother, given his schedule. And we recalled the unique demands we experienced as the lone black faculty member, managing administrative, teaching and scholarship responsibilities while advising and mentoring students. The CUNY job was very attractive. Chancellor Robert Kibbee's commitment to access and passion to help students who had been underserved were undisputed. The Board of Trustees voted unanimously to approve my appointment. I was honored to be part of his team and was humbled in knowing I had been selected from a pool of more than 300 candidates.

In my four years at Claremont, I had developed the program to respond to new state teacher education guidelines, created new courses in multicultural education, established the joint public-private doctoral program, edited the *California Journal on Teacher Education*, completed several articles, participated in and led statewide meetings, enrolled in a postdoctoral summer program in Washington D.C., and guided more than a dozen doctoral dissertations. As I was leaving, Clyde Curran, professor of philosophy at the graduate school, took three paintings off his wall and presented them to me. I gave John Regan the easel from my office, and I accepted with gratitude his praise of the depth of my academic contribution. The academy was losing a scholar to administration, he said. His words were a wonderful gift.

The doctoral students I worked with were a special support and regarded my good fortune as theirs. Margo Long took the lead in planning parties and helping me pack up. As a white Jewish woman married to a black man, Margo had found in my classes a group of friends who appreciated her level of enlightenment. She spoke of her children as black and shared her intention to expose them to the richness of their black heritage as well as to Jewish traditions. It was Margo who took the lead in the students' joining together to create a huge quilt of 12 individual squares expressing their unique perspectives, perspectives that came together in a whole of earth colors and a breathtaking vibrance. It was a gift for my wall from beyond Claremont.

This same group of students encouraged me to select one of them as my executive assistant in my new job in New York. "Who will be your Sancho, as you, Don Quixote, surge ahead?" one asked. I was able to persuade Dennis Cabral, a white male of Portuguese background from Hawaii, to take the job as my executive assistant. I had learned from Dennis the impact of discrimination experienced by the rural poor of Hawaii whose families worked on sugar cane plantations. As a child he fantasized about becoming invisible. He did not want to become invisible as an adult. He felt deeply that no one had the right, through the use of words, to make anyone invisible, as he saw what labels could do to a child's self-esteem. It would be Dennis on whom I would count to help me maintain a congruence between myself and my role as an administrator.

The move to New York was a different matter for Jane. To her thinking, I was out of control and had abandoned my role as a mother and wife. It was yet another move in her life of moves from coast to coast. She had settled on my being the problem in her agony of having to separate herself from her friends and bearing the brunt of social and geographic changes. Her bond with her father was strong. He had taught her how to drive, ride a bike and ice-skate. She had accompanied him as he learned to fly small airplanes. These were important milestones and pleasures. I was breaking things up.

She gained some insight into my predicament as she realized her father would not continue as principal. Without my new job, we might have to use some of the funds she had saved for her trip to Kenya to pay bills. Yet moving and being uprooted were not a solutions to her. Her feelings came to a head as she and I were in her room packing for her trip to Kenya. As she packed she realized she would not be returning to our spacious ranch house, with its view of the mountains, on Radcliffe Road. Her venting began with accusations that I was destroying the family. She didn't know what was going on. "All you care about is yourself," she said.

It did no good for me to counter with how going to New York would mean I would be tripling my salary and be in a position to support two children in college. "Look ahead at what you will have a chance to do," I told her. She threw a pillow at me, and then another. I returned the pillows with equal force. We swung the pillows at each other, until they were out of our reach, and then we began throwing her clothes, flinging them at each other and about the room and crying until our tears turned to laughter.

I realized in that encounter how much I had left to chance in raising her as I grew up. I had chanced that her future would be secured by her fair skin, wavy hair, pretty face, intelligence and the advantage of material things. I had not given to her what had been given to me by strong black women. In their wisdom my grandmothers had provided me a mother-idea in which mothers take the lead in moving the family from slavery to freedom and from freedom to economic independence. Fathers are present, yet the realities of racism often-times make them shadowy figures.

In some ways I had treated Jane as a white princess. Yet, like me, she knew who she was. Her skin color had not confused her. But I had disadvantaged her by not creating for her experiences to learn from her elders. We had traveled too far from the starting point of culture. I knew I could not address

this fact in a moment. I would have to be vigilant in letting her
see me, warts and all. It would be the magic of time that I had
to count on.

Leaving California did not seem to me as my farewell to
my husband. We would, I felt, find our way back to each other
despite the damage being done to our marriage in the circumstances of our separation. Tom would be living with another
woman. I would initially be going to New York City alone. We
confessed our love for each other. At the same time, he was
clear that it would be difficult for him to go to New York in the
position of carrying my coat. He needed to be economically
independent as well. I held my thoughts about how it was
okay for me for so many years to be instrumental to his
advancement. Besides, I wanted to prove to him, as well as to
others, that I could carry my own coat, thank you very much.

Tom took me to the airport in Ontario, California. Our
eyes filled with tears as we said goodbye. From my window
seat, I watched him—tall, arms folded, eyes blinking as the
plane revved to get ready to soar East. I was 41 and about to
live alone for the first time in my life in New York City while
serving as the City University of New York's first black female
vice chancellor.

MILE 17

Are the legs sturdy and developed enough to carry the runner a long distance? Are the arms and back strong enough for her to reach ever forward?

Landing in New York thrust me into the center of controversy. The *New York Times* ran a story about my appointment headlined, "Californian Gets the Job." The article went on to say how members of the New York State Legislative Black Caucus had severed their ties with CUNY Chancellor Kibbee over my appointment. Caucus members had two issues: first, they felt the new Board of Trustees guidelines for special programs were meant to restrict access even more, and second; they felt that someone from California, unfamiliar with New York's issues, would not be responsive to the concerns of the minority community.

As a first step, I had to make sure the Caucus understood my commitment. I turned to Al Vann, a member of the state legislature and a Caucus member. I'd known Al from my teaching days in Brooklyn and parties we would have in Jersey. Realizing that my approach to him might have been strengthened with Tom present, I anticipated his asking where Tom was in my move. Had I left him behind? Was I putting him aside or stepping ahead? Was my appointment yet another example of white men passing over black men by appointing a black woman? I knew that while a friendship with Al Vann was important, it was the results that would matter.

My new colleagues at the central office were not pleased that I'd be bringing in an executive assistant of my choice rather than selecting one of their suggestions who was familiar with CUNY. It was a legitimate concern. I agreed with the need to have someone as second-in-command who knew the system and with whom I could work, someone with both a sense of purpose and a sense of humor. I found that person in

124

Leo Corbie, who was director of special programs at one of the senior colleges. In a meeting of special program directors, I observed the respect the other program directors had for Leo and appreciated the passion with which he talked about students. "The students are the reason I am here," he said. And he walked his talk. Leo was also someone who knew the strengths and weaknesses of all the players. He accepted the position of deputy vice chancellor of student affairs and special programs.

To my delight, I was invited to present my academic portfolio. I was granted tenure as professor in education at Brooklyn College. That was a treasure.

As a team, Leo, Dennis and I worked together to learn the budget process, map out how we wanted to implement the guidelines for special programs and plan a strategy to coordinate the centralization of admissions and financial aid for CUNY's 18 colleges.

We had to hit the ground running and be aggressive in developing relationships with legislators, trustees, members of the chancellor's cabinet, college presidents and student support personnel. This meant we had to be open in what we did not know, yet at the same time be clear about what we wanted to achieve.

The budget was a major challenge. The team in the budget office was energetic, bright and no-nonsense in the expectation that you had to figure out ways to get the flexibility you needed. I knew it would help to win them over by developing a relationship with them. Watching their Friday night volleyball games in an area adjacent to the central office, I decided to offer the budget office a volleyball game challenge against the office of student affairs and special programs.

I lined up a team who, like me, had no experience. Dennis, Leo and I began to talk up what we were going to do to the team in the budget office. We had shirts printed. One side read, "The Budget Stops Here," and the other side, "The Three C's" for Cross, Corbie and Cabral. We lost game after game and declared we would not leave the court until we had won one. Nighttime settled in and we continued to lose. But we had won. We had turned a page in our relationship with our budget colleagues.

Getting attention in the cabinet meetings was another challenge. My Claremont Graduate School approach didn't work in New York. I could see that my mini-speeches about access, mission and diversity weren't pulling me into the group. I listened as other vice chancellors talked in technical terms or jargon familiar to them. Occasionally they would be discussing areas where I had program responsibility as if I weren't there. It was clear that being around the table didn't mean you were automatically involved in the discussion.

The situation changed somewhat when, after hearing the group go on and on about the technicalities related to direct admissions, I asked: "Why do we have direct admits?" The deputy chancellor responded, "Good question!" and smiled as if I had just arrived and not been there for months. I had learned an important New York lesson: a thoughtful question is more appreciated than the right answer.

It was my father who took on the role of educating me about other New York nuances. We had seen each other occasionally over the years. I had kept up with his activities through my sister, with whom he regularly played cards, and through his sister, my Aunt Carolyn. He had moved over a period of years from Harlem to Brooklyn to Southhold, Long Island, and then to the Bronx, where he was living with his third or fourth wife.

Charlie took to coming by every Saturday morning to enjoy a good cigar and bring a sugary breakfast. He began each visit with an inspection of my refrigerator and express amazement that I could exist with such bare shelves. "Baby, you have the only apartment in New York City where roaches starve to death," he'd say. He listened as I talked about the challenges in the new job. Nothing I said sounded unusual to him. He seemed to expect it to be that way, tough to get into. It took a while for me to get his message. He'd say things like: "Have you ever been to the West Side of the city?" "Remember that restaurant I used to take you and your sister to in Harlem?" or "Do you still know how to roller-skate?" After some time, I realized my father was saying, get a life, enjoy yourself a bit more. At times he'd be quite direct, come right out, "Baby, I'm proud of you but don't be so serious all the time."

Unlike my mother, my father did not view my having returned to New York alone as my failing in marriage. He had associated himself with strong black women as a matter of course and had no doubts about my finding my way. He liked having me to himself on those Saturdays. I realized how I had missed him and enjoyed the traits we shared. We both stuttered when we got excited or nervous and were of the same brown skin tone. And we shared a flair for dressing. He'd laugh when I'd comment: "I don't remember you ever having hair. Got any pictures?" What he enjoyed most was the opportunity to be my escort. He knew how to tell a good joke and flirt.

I shared my new life with my mother as well. I invited her to a reception at Chancellor Kibbee's. At first she was tentative, reverting to a shyness she could put on with whites. She worried about her presence, her dress, her hair and her shoes. The chancellor picked up on her shyness and reached out to include her by asking her to make a few remarks.

She began quietly, thanking him for the opportunity and for being so welcoming to her daughter, Dr. Cross. Then I noticed her brow go up, a signal to anyone who knew her well that Ozie was in gear. She ignored my signals. "Be cool, Ma, keep it short," I gestured through my face and hands. She turned to her audience and began a review of the issues facing the black community in America, why welfare made a difference and the importance of Social Security. To my dread, she then went into her views on the "cheese conspiracy." To her thinking the government was creating a major health problem in the black community by distributing free cheese to welfare recipients. I noticed the shifting of feet in the room as she continued for what was approaching 10 minutes. The mood and her speech were broken by a light applause, which in my mind was meant to end it and in her mind, to affirm her speech. She laughed and smiled and was very pleased with herself. After that, I was frequently asked about my mother, sometimes with concern.

I loved the energy of Manhattan. Despite being from Newark and having taught in Brooklyn, the city dazzled me. I was experiencing the city like Dorothy from Kansas. During my first week, when I saw a horde of people coming out from a subway station, my first impression was of a parade. And after years of being car-dependent in California, I loved being without a car. I would walk the three miles between my apartment and the office on East 80th Street. I spent so much time on the East side of New York, that I took my father's advice and spent some of Thanksgiving break on the West side.

It had been close to ten years since I had lived on the East Coast, but I found myself relating very quickly to the leadership role the City University of New York had taken in promoting access for eligible students. CUNY's statement was one being made for all of urban higher education. I felt the connection with my growing up in Newark's rich ethnic collage. Yet I was reminded in a curious way that urban blacks of my generation were not expected to be showing the way as vice chancellors. At a cocktail reception, a senior colleague approached me with the question: "Where are you from? From the islands? Which one? Are you from the South? Which state? Well, were you raised in California, where you had been on the faculty? Then are you from someplace Upstate?" I'd answer a quiet "no," as he sought to place me. And then finally I responded: "I am from Newark, New Jersey. Like you, I have my roots in urban areas and attended Queens College of CUNY." I did not imagine what I read in his face. He did not expect me, someone with urban roots much like his, to be there. I wished I had reminded him of the thousands of young black men and women with potential and determination who made it and of the many thousands more to whom we were morally obligated to give a chance.

The dilemma as I saw it in 1978 was a failure to believe in one's gut that young black people who are products of the harshness of urban life can survive it all and make a credible statement. They can transcend their environment. They can do what is necessary to go the distance. They can redefine themselves and work beside sons and daughters of immigrants, white liberals, as equal players. All are players helping others and themselves, flushed and glowing from exertion.

Mile 17.7

You've established a base in training hard and in staying focused. You're a runner. Enjoy the moment. Feel it. Sense a moving ahead, a staying ahead. Keep up. Cheer yourself on. Try not to look back to see who is gaining on you.

Your body remembers.

As a black woman with a history that includes my mother's story and the story of so many who went before me, at some point I had to make a decision about how best to handle the tugs and pulls from my husband, family and friends wanting me to relate to their individual pain. Being in New York as vice chancellor and seeing how I was related to the big picture propelled me forward. I felt I might play a part both in addressing their collective despair and contributing to providing real opportunities for the underserved and disadvantaged. I found myself communicating all I knew from personal and professional experience. I could be in company with the moment and still surge ahead. Yet when I hesitated, slowed my pace, I felt a yearning to look back. I wrote at the time in my journal:

> The body remembers when I was not alone, but with Tom. The body remembers his soothing my despair, his touches, strokes and closing out of absurdities. So many times he'd say some things don't matter. So often I'd feel with his caress that nothing else should matter. But it doesn't work.
>
> The body remembers his being the strength of his children, letting them be young, helping them grow while being subjected to the cruelest stereotype of all, the stallion athlete.
>
> The body remembers him as simply a man who perceived the revolution as the maintenance of self and the black family. And the body remembers his being angry

without the pain showing, a warrior.

The body remembers his being my friend, our having to wear masks and reach out for affirmation.

The body remembers the pain of moving ahead.

The conflicts in moving ahead were always present. When I told Tom I needed to be instrumental to others and at the same time help the family, he heard me saying, "others are more important than I am to you." He grew sad and frightened. I felt his sense of powerlessness as he saw me expanding my role and responsibility. It was as if I had created a burden that he too must carry. My steps ahead of him created dust that obscured our views of each other. We were growing faint to each other.

On one level our marriage ended because it was gutsy and fashionable in the late 1970s and early 1980s for women to "do." On another level, our marriage ended because I had created a fictional "all in one" husband whom I expected to work with me in changing the diapers and changing the world. It was a bit of both, yet it was less complicated to blame the collapse of our marriage on the "other woman." My fantasy was that in my having done good and made a contribution, my husband would move from strength to strength and love me heroically and unconditionally. In 1979, I wrote and received the following:

Dear Tom,

Please understand what I'm about to say.

You're back in California with B. We should get a divorce and mend our relationships with the children. I want an opportunity to put my own life together and to figure things out.

I love you and always will, but I don't want to renew the commitment. I just want to go it alone. You're right. I have had my flings, yet miss being with you. And I won't be foolish and try to work something out just to be in your company. Tom, you don't want to face the reality of where you are and the impact of your involvement with B. Our marriage has eroded. The confusion deepens for both of us. We should seek a divorce.

Then, you must get a job. If you were here, we'd be at each other again and neither of us wants that. It can't work for now because I don't want to work at it.

B. loves you and you care for her. It is not the same as our relationship, but it is a relationship that must be accepted because it exists and it must be accepted by our kids, our family and friends. One impression should be corrected. The relationship with B. did not create the problem. It uncovered some problems, our going different ways, changes in my life and changes that must be made as we adjust to our having two children in college.

I did care, do love you, but we seem to be destructive to each other in ways we never were before.
Dolores

Dear Dolores:

We have experienced some loving wonderful times. It is an understatement to say that I/we have enjoyed them. These times of sharing, caring and intimacy are us. What I want to express is that for the times we do have we should minimize the blockage and distortions that are there. I don't need a hell of a lot of time. It is not that complicated. This really entails dropping the defenses and being honest at the "I can help resolve stage" and taking real ownership for the outcome.

We spend more time on incidentals to the relationship than the relationship itself. I want to be with you and I love you. But if we can't try, I guess I must rest the effort.
Tom

We approached the divorce as if it were another move, another adventure for two people who had tried and succeeded in everything else. As with other decisions, we didn't talk it out with friends and family. They suspected we were living on the edge in our marriage, yet they felt we would work it out. We were "Tom and Dee."

We talked about being divorced and then at some point remarrying. We came together at my apartment to sign the divorce papers and spoke of how civilized our proceedings would be compared with the battles and fights we'd observed in other divorcing friends. We talked as well about how the timing of our divorce was more thoughtful to our kids because they were in college and on their way to being on their own. We had been good parents. We were doing a no-fault divorce and playing it all to ourselves as the audience.

I chided Tom for bringing me coffee with milk, not black, and went on to say he must be confusing me with someone else, her preference. We kidded each other and took a sentimental journey, speaking of how the signing of divorce papers reminded us of all the details in the purchase of our first home in Lakeview.

We spoke of how in time we would undo what we were doing in signing the divorce papers and recalled celebrities who married former spouses. Tom began to cry, "Dee what are we doing?" I cried and buried my head in his shoulder. We were moving ahead, riding some wave, but we couldn't hide the sadness.

When I was alone later that evening, I thought of the children's book *Where Do Butterflies Go When It Rains?* I felt the vulnerability of aloneness.

We had not discussed the divorce with our children. Jane was at UC Davis and Tom Jr. was at Sonoma State University. We had sketched out our problems but not covered them in depth. They expected us to pull things together, even as they heard me becoming more strident. They also had seen me wistful in the presence of other men and had known of Tom's relationship with B. I wrote them when the divorce was final, six weeks after our signing:

Dear Tommy and Jane:
     This is the first letter I am writing you as a single woman. The divorce has happened. I learned that it was final today. I feel tired, a bit sad, and unsure about what it'll all mean. The past few weeks have been confusing

emotionally and you know of our going back and forth.

Briefly, I wanted to get your father back. We wrote and we both suffered. I wanted him here to be with me as I entered the new job and it irked him to know I was turning to others for support. I was also hurt to know that Dad was with someone else being comforted. That's been tough. Yet to my friends, I have not said a word about what's been going on, which in itself doesn't make sense.

Last night Dad advised me to find someone else. Today notice of the divorce. Can love have been and yet completely not be? If I am so great, how could I lose? It's all so reckless. He's wounded and will find someone to tend his wounds and become his guardian. Perhaps, what I was doing largely was testing: Would he scale walls and come after me? I've been the super black woman, making a contribution to her family, inspiring and working for him, and for so long making things happen for my "Man of LaMancha."

The divorce means that we, that is, your father and I, will speak of each other differently and that will be difficult for you both. You will hear me as you do now putting my spin on things, yet questioning.

We are not a family in the way we were, yet some things will not change: the respect I have for your father and he for me and our love for you, our children. The relationship of parent to child does not change.

So what went wrong, honestly? Well, within a few lines, it is like this: Dad has a tendency to piss on himself (that is not to fully deal with the reality of being a black man in America and not to use his strengths to take a stand for what matters most).

When I couldn't stop him, shock him, get him to stop wetting on himself, I started to piss on him like everyone else. And let that be a lesson to you. Don't piss on yourself. If you're caught wetting your pants, others will piss on you. All to say, in what is a vulgar way, I share a responsibility for the divorce and what has happened. It is difficult to resist looking back, again and again. From anxiety came confusion, separation and the divorce.
I love you both, Mom

Jane responded:

Dear Mom,

Well here's your official moral support letter. It's really prompt because I don't want to hear you've been moping all around the city freaking out because Dad has not got his act together. Now, you have been very sensitive and giving in your recent relations with Dad. You've been humane even to the point of acting irrationally, i.e. supporting him and asking him back. Now Mom you shouldn't do things like that. This is not time to back track. Your marital relationship with Dad is over. Please try to face that. What I want you to do is to get over those feelings of inadequacy that make you want to cling to Dad. Then get over those feelings of pity that make you want to help Dad so much.

It's different for women today. Get with the program. Think very highly of yourself and look out for yourself, or Dad will just use your compassion to his benefit. That's just the way he is. I'm one of the few people, perhaps the only person, who know how much pain and anguish Dad has put you through. Don't look back at the times when the marriage worked. Look at right now and honestly ask yourself is it emotionally and financially wise to stay attached to Dad.

And for Pete's sake, stop vacillating. You have decided what to do. You had good reasons for it. You know why you had to go through with your decisions. This was for real. I know you're strong enough to survive.

You'll find being divorced is not easy but remember staying together is not reasonable or feasible. You two have your own lives. Live them.

You're finally getting your life together. No, I don't believe you'll be lonely. Do not let your preoccupation with companionship make you chained to Dad.

Please stay strong for Tommy and me. We both love you very much. I'm upset that I can't be there to help give you support but you know where to call if you really feel down. Keep it up. You're on the right track. Listen to that song on the *Pippin* album, "Extraordinary," because that's

what you are. I'm rooting for you.
Love, Jane.

I recognized in Jane's communication with me the role reversal, as she supported me as if she were the mother and encouraged me to stay the course. I thought back to the play *for colored girls*, and the strength and independence of those black women. They were women who were free of the "walk softly behind your man" attitude of my generation, who all too often apologized for their achievements.

At some point black women, indeed all women, come to terms with needing more, with the knowledge that making a contribution to their men, their families and being there isn't enough. They need to be able to stretch out on every level: emotional, spiritual, physical and intellectual and embrace what they aspire to do unashamedly.

> The body remembers when as a young baby I smiled, stretched and felt my mother's breast.
>
> The body remembers being alone to deal with fantasies that took me on glorious voyages, tamed the disquiet and dealt with my discontent.
>
> The body remembers stepping alone and not slipping, not losing what is me.
>
> The body remembers being in touch with a younger Dee, bold, ambitious, confident and unafraid.
>
> And the body remembers strutting my stuff, creating energy, developing defenses and taking on the hurdles that spring from my blackness, my gender and economic circumstance.

MILE 18.2

We're ahead of the pack, moving quickly up the hill. I accept that Heidi is faster. I need her to set the pace as I visualize the two of us as elite runners leading the way and knowing that others will have to find their pace. It's a training run. The runners behind us grumble, complain that we've moved ahead.

The trainer bounds ahead and beckons us to stop. He then turns to me as if I'd started it all and begins to chastise me for finding a pace and being in a space ahead of the other runners. We move out again. I'm moving out yet weighed down by what has occurred.

I am aware of being the only black runner in the group. I was singled out as the problem, yet Heidi, a white female, was leading the group. I keep moving, vowing to stay centered. The run has been made harder but I will keep going.

GOVERNOR CAREY NAMES 3 WOMEN TO HIGH LEVEL POSITIONS

ALBANY, Dec. 11— Governor Carey today nominated three women for high level assignments in his administration...[including] Dr. Dolores E. Cross of New York City to president of the New York State Higher Education Services Corporation. The appointments must now be confirmed by the Senate. —*The New York Times*, Friday, Dec. 12, 1980

The move would make me the highest-ranking black woman in New York state government and among the top in the nation. The agency I would administer provided more than $2 billion a year in financial aid to 750,000 New Yorkers. While the other two appointees in the article were confirmed within a relatively short period of time, it would be five months before my confirmation hearing.

The subject of my confirmation would come up on most

social occasions, expanding my insights on the process and the politics. At a party in Brooklyn, I was seated next to Ted Jackson, a black male and Executive Vice President of the Bowery Savings Bank. He asked "Why do you think the Governor offered you the job?" I replied, "Because I am qualified." He swallowed in obvious disbelief at my response and said, "Indeed," and smiled. He alluded to his friendship with some of the legislators and made it clear that some of the Republicans were not pleased with my being nominated by the governor. I would need Caucus support, he said. The job was clearly political, he added, and there would be those out there who would be trying to find some reason not to appoint me. I liked his apparent candor, but I wondered if he could be trusted. Had he been sent to check me out? I recalled the advice of friends who wasted no time in telling me: "Dee, you're in New York now. Things have changed. You have to check these guys out." And again, I went back to my grandmother's wisdom: "Take everyone's advice but use your own judgment." I needed someone secure, knowledgeable and, on the face of it, interested in my success. I also sought someone I could rely on, a friend who understood that while the confirmation involved me personally, there were bigger issues. My appointment had been an "in your face" move to the Black Caucus. The governor made the appointment without consulting with them. And I would have to discreetly become their choice in what I did from that point on. I also was aware that the people around the governor didn't really think I was going to run the agency. It was a processing operation. They envisioned that I'd do the annual reports and let the "technicians" run the operation. As with the position of vice chancellor, I was going to the New York State Higher Education Services Corporation in Albany as an outsider and an unknown quantity in state government.

I began to use and create social occasions to speak to what I'd been achieving in my two years at CUNY. People needed to know that I had an agenda and was not just talking about the problems but solving them. I had succeeded in getting the chancellor to convene the presidents of all the colleges to involve them in implementing guidelines for the operation of special programs in their respective colleges. And I visited all the colleges, obtained their plans and documented their progress. The objective was to make sure that underserved students with potential and determination would be given a chance to succeed. A Board of Trustees committee on Special Programs and Student Affairs was created to monitor and support the activities of the office, and financial aid officers were involved in assessing the impact of federal guidelines. I provided information to the Black Caucus and other legislators interested in the CUNY issues. I developed a script focused on the issues and on actions. I was actualizing the advice I'd given to my Claremont students, namely the importance of achieving a connection between your role and your person. There was little doubt about my commitment and my perspective that young people with potential must be given a chance if we are serious about improving the quality of life for a diverse population. I'd also been clear about my willingness to take risks by articulating my concerns in professional and community meetings and before the Budget Committee in Albany. Within a relatively short time, I had taken a leadership role in the centralization of CUNY's financial aid system.

While I chose to view my advocacy and seriousness of purpose as positive, not everyone was pleased with my determination not to let the office of student affairs and special programs be marginalized. It was suggested to me on one occasion that some of my detractors in the central office collaborated to move me on to state government given my proactive, firm approach to making sure the office was effective in promoting access and first-class opportunities for CUNY's diverse population.

I viewed the statewide office as an opportunity to take my advocacy efforts to yet another level while maintaining my momentum and direction.

I would not let the work and disillusionment sap my energy. We had to keep going. In the 1950s we'd been buoyed by the *Brown* decision and won and lost some battles. In the 1960s we'd experienced a short decade of enlightenment that led to changes in law, specifically the Higher Education Act, which provided financial aid. In the 1970s we saw more minorities have the opportunity to go on to graduate school and the development of support programs. Now, in 1980, we were aware of running in place because of the many threats to access to higher education.

It was time for me to move on. I needed to gather information and involve others in improving the delivery of financial aid. Key to this improvement was analyzing the impact of financial aid on the opportunities for individuals in the public and independent schools and the interaction of financial aid with race, gender and economic circumstance.

MILE 19

When I get tired of running alone, and there's a stretch to go, I visualize someone running with me, most often a relative, living or dead. I find myself talking to them or remembering something encouraging they've done. It keeps me going.

For my mother, my nomination to the presidency of the agency was the answer to her prayers. She was enrolled full time at Union College in New Jersey and needed some help in unraveling the financial aid process. She also was deeply concerned about the grace period allowed before a borrower was considered to be in default. She had seen many of her young student friends denied access to financial aid because they had a loan default on their record. In one breath she hoped I wouldn't work too hard, and in the next she'd give me a list of issues to resolve.

My father wondered what might happen to our Saturdays together. He was deeply pleased when I told him of my plans to return to New York City on the weekends. He smiled and said: "Henry wouldn't be a bit surprised. He loved you so much that I had to remind him more than once that you're my daughter."

My father then told me that he had found Henry living on the streets of New York. "We don't take care of family like we used to," he said. "Henry never had his own place, but he had always been able to find a bed. By the time I found him, TB had set in, and there was no place for him but the hospital. He didn't last long after that."

My father gave me $50 and told me to buy a dress when I took a holiday trip to be with Jane in Spain. I did not expect that our conversation that Saturday would be our last. Jane and I were shopping in Barcelona, the Saturday after Christmas, when I saw a dress to buy with the money he gave me. It was a dark green tunic dress, embroidered in gold. At dinner that evening, I told Jane I felt a sense of urgency to return home earlier than scheduled. Upon arriving at Kennedy Airport there was the message for me to call my sister, Jean. I called and learned that Dad had suffered a heart attack and died the same Saturday I purchased the dress. After an hour of crying inconsolably, I changed into the dark green tunic in an airport restroom. I didn't want to go home, as I knew there would be a note from him. Whenever I went out of town, he would visit my apartment, straighten something out and leave a note for me.

Daddy was into people, laughter and fun, and he always wanted me to have more light times. I remembered a friend's annual party, so I made my way there and became a part of the event. When I returned home, I found my father's note of seven words, "Baby I did the best I could." He was referring to sweeping some things out for me. I read it as so much more. My father was 61 when he died. I'd gained a great deal in our Saturdays together. He viewed my accepting the position in Albany as a gamble. It didn't matter if I won or lost, it was important that I took the risk. Gambling, he said, was in my blood. No matter what happened in Albany, I'd take a chance again and again. It pleased him that he'd passed that on to me.

MILE 20

What does the race mean? Staying ahead, being with others, hanging in there, taking one step and then the other. Each step exacts a toll, yet I have prepared and trained for every footfall. The pace is mine. The race is mine. I own the process it took to get here, one that includes workouts and the fantasies and realities of pushing ahead.

I began the job as president of the New York State Higher Education Services Corporation (HESC) in early 1981, a time when many of us in the higher education community were becoming increasingly concerned about proposed cuts in Title IV student aid programs. This would mean radical changes in federal support for needy students. It signaled a definite retreat from the country's long-standing commitment to supporting access to postsecondary education. I knew from my experience in the City University of New York that many key policymakers did not recognize the absolutely vital role that student financial aid played in making postsecondary education a reality. To restrict aid would dash the hopes of many, and much potential would remain unfilled.

At the same time, New York had been a leader in state grant programs. New York's tuition assistance program accounted for one-third of the total funds in all need-based state grant programs in the nation. I also realized that of prime concern to the legislators in the state was providing financial aid to their constituents. I viewed my task as adding to what was known on the importance of financial aid to access, adding to what was known about paying for college and, at the same time, improving the delivery of financial aid to New Yorkers.

The agency had gone through a series of crises during its early years, which had earned it bad press and a poor image. The problems related to the agency's inability to process student aid applications on a timely basis. When I assumed top job, the agency was chugging along, having improved its aid processing and delivering aid to students. I felt very strongly that the role of a state agency was not only to provide services but also to disseminate information on the impact of its services to legislators, college presidents and students and their parents. This would require greatly expanding efforts in financial aid research and financial aid information.

I brought a personal agenda to the agency. I had struggled for many years to achieve my educational aspirations and knew first hand the hardships of low-income and minority students. I had come from a family that was unable to provide me any financial help in my college years. It had taken me close to nine years to complete my undergraduate education going to school a mixture of full- and part-time. Moreover, without information, you couldn't fulfill your dreams. There were students in junior and senior high school who simply had not been advised that financial aid was available and believed that college was not an option.

As a divorced parent, I knew well the weight of supporting children in college alone. I was having to plan and make adjustments to support Tom and Jane in college. In Albany, as I made adjustments to handle the expenses my children were incurring in college, I went from a small apartment to a rooming house to a place over a liquor store to a basement apartment to a second-flat apartment over the course of eight years. In addition, I carried Plus Loans and they had student loans. But my sacrifice dimmed in comparison with what other parents with fewer resources had to make.

How best could I tell the story? All families were experiencing difficulties, some more than others. And many parents, lawmakers and college presidents honestly felt the neediest were getting a free ride. I knew from my conversations with financial aid advisors at CUNY that this simply was not the case. Many students with full-aid packages were having to drop out or stop out, citing a shortfall in funds as a barrier to continuing.

I drew on the legislated mandate for the agency, that is, to promote access to postsecondary education for all eligible students through the administration of financial aid. I would interpret its mission broadly. It was my good fortune to have the support of existing leadership at HESC. They were ready to take risks, take giant steps, and not be captive of "the way it had been done in the past." There were colleagues there who felt the depth of the agency's mission and wanted to keep it alive in spite of politics: Michael Cruskie, Peter Keitel and Frank Hynes.

I asked myself what my uncles had asked of me: "What do your actions mean to the community? How are you helping the underserved?" I would not permit my values to be compromised. The response by legislators, even some of the same skin hue as mine, was to subject me to slights and demonstrations of disrespect. On more than one occasion, they arrived late to meetings I had called or they simply didn't show up. One introduced me in a large public forum as "a lovely lady."

To avoid wearing myself down, I learned to make early exits and take action to guard my values. I avoided parties where legislators tried to prey on me for a deal, or excused myself because of my early morning runs. I needed to maintain my spirit.

And I found in my secretary, Barbara McAdoo, someone who would use her personal experience to assure me that I was on the right track. Barbara McAdoo is a remarkable black woman who literally raised seven children on her own and another half-dozen grandchildren. She helped me focus, and in a firm way, she protected me as I tended to want to make time for everyone.

I began immediately to work on transforming the agency's culture. The agency was relatively small, with fewer than 1,000 employees in a single location. I held "getting-to-know-you" receptions in every department. I talked about the mission and its meaning. "This is not just another civil service job. We're on a mission," I said. And I spoke to them of the larger picture, how federal cutbacks might affect the agency and make our work both more crucial and more complex.

I added a training specialist to the personnel department and identified an internal auditor who would report directly to me. Most important, Barbara helped me maintain a schedule of regular visits to offices and alerted me to special occasions for employees and opportunities to congratulate individuals for their accomplishments. I also found ways to get the staff out socializing together on company picnics, holiday parties and regularly scheduled softball games. Instead of following a reactive mode, I took a proactive stance in moving the organization forward.

A good relationship with financial aid administrators in the state was key. Any research and improvements in getting information out relied on them. I reached out to form a committee of financial aid administrators and appointed a HESC administrator as a liaison to the financial aid administrator's statewide organization. Governor Carey agreed to convene a committee of 21 college presidents on the agency's behalf. This group helped us learn how best to convey the role of financial aid to their colleagues. And they were ready spokespeople to provide testimony on the detrimental impact of proposed cutbacks in financial aid.

The HESC Office of Research undertook a statewide survey—the first of its kind in the nation—to get more information on how financial aid recipients and those who didn't get financial aid were financing their education. A major focus of the survey was to determine if students ran short of funds for their education and whether these shortfalls were more prevalent among particular types of students. We found that, for many financial aid recipients, the dollars received did not fully cover educational costs, even when combined with a family contribution specified in the aid formula. To make up for this shortfall, families had to contribute more than was expected, and students had to work more. The hardest hit were the financially independent students. These students were more likely to be members of a minority group, older, and to have children. These were young men and women on their own, eligible for college and intent on creating a better life for themselves and their children. Any reduction in government aid would adversely affect the educational aspirations of those who were the most dependent on financial aid, namely, minorities and women, and this reduction could create a legacy of undereducated people for generations yet to come.

Any cutback would send a negative message to potential students. They would be discouraged. So our agency proceeded to take a lead role in making more information available to colleges and students about paying for college. I initiated a regular talk show about paying for college, where I answered questions from callers. The agency devised a student financial aid estimator system that would permit students and parents to input information and get an estimate on financial aid they would receive.

The information from the survey revealed the necessity for aid to part-time students. The data showed, for example, that when students had to drop from full-time attendance to part time they faced the hardship of paying tuition. Some ultimately dropped out. I formed a committee and held roundtable discussions throughout the state to share this information and get concerned individuals to become advocates for aid to part-time students. We succeeded. Legislation was passed to provide financial aid to students enrolled at least 6 hours per term.

Drawing on a program started by a private benefactor, Eugene Lang, which supported students from seventh grade through their graduation from college, I proposed to Governor Cuomo the establishment of Liberty Scholarships. These scholarships served as an incentive for students as early as the seventh grade to stay in school and work hard. The premise was simple and grounded on research: when young people are told in a straightforward manner that their college expenses will be paid for, they will stay in high school, graduate and go on to college.

It was important to provide hope, I wrote in an issues paper. The world was becoming dependent on people who could adapt to technological change, but we had not added incentives to keep students in the education pipeline. Now was the time.

I also began to court the media, creating a public relations office and hiring a former TV newswoman, Dencye Duncan Lacy, to head the operation. She organized press conferences on the survey results and arranged for me to make TV appearances and even to host a regular interview show on a cable station in New York City.

All the while, there continued to be critics who systematically denied the realities that we uncovered. My response was to keep pushing, using the strength of my position and the reality of my experience to counter indifferent and uncaring economic and political forces.

As president of HESC, I had to shift and start over and over again as various proposals came forth that would constrict access to higher education, either by regulations that made the process of getting financial aid more difficult or by cutbacks that would make even fewer dollars available. The accompanying Liberty Partnerships provided help in the form of mentoring and academic support at the high school level, where New York State was losing up to 40 percent of its students. In 1984, only 47 percent of black students and 43 percent of Hispanic students in grades 9 through 12 were still in school.

Even bad news that would make financial aid appear too unpredictable was a factor to combat. When discouragement set in among my staff, the task for me became cheering my staff on with their impact on the mission. We had to keep focusing on the importance of what we were doing. At the same time, we had to show more than passion. We had to counter myths with data and to keep on presenting facts to colleagues in higher education, to policymakers, and to students and their parents in a way that kept them focused on the larger picture. For New York, the larger picture was the importance of student financial aid in maintaining a diverse workforce and maintaining the state's leadership role as an advocate for promoting access to postsecondary education through financial aid to all eligible students.

While I contacted the media to celebrate the state's leadership role in providing financial aid to needy students and to get the word out about the great unmet financial need among potential students, I realized reporters were equally interested in the time students were taking to complete their degrees. People were becoming concerned about the tax dollars supporting students who, on the face of it, did not appear to be serious, as judged by the length of time it was taking for them to earn their degrees and the high loan-default rates of some students.

There were few people of color in this country in leadership positions, people who had as a frame of reference the reality of suffering through Jim Crow laws, hearing their parents speak of walking miles to elementary schools and in some cases not having the opportunity to go on even to high school. Many of our leaders had not seen firsthand people with darker skins being relegated to the lowest forms of service. Nor did many know at the gut level that equity had not been addressed to the point where families could make up the unmet financial needs to send their talented children to college. Not addressing access had scared, confused and frustrated a host of people. Those of us in leadership had to keep pushing, had to appear bigger than life in making our case.

On weekends, I took the Amtrak train from Albany to New York City, where I had an apartment in Stuyvesant town. Each click of the train wheels on the track added up to a melody heralding time to myself. At times I caught up with Ted for dinner or a movie. But he found me absorbed, unable to disconnect from my life in Albany. "Does your activity give you any more satisfaction than your sister Jean's gives her? Are you really happy?" he asked.

I thought of my sister's bubbly style, her time for jigsaw puzzles, card games and excursions to Atlantic City. She always made time to have fun. Ted wasn't the only one who kept urging me to "lighten up, girl." "Can't ever find you" and "When you gonna find some time for us?" were mainstays of my conversations with friends. But I wasn't interested; I did not want to be caught up in their lifestyles. I was intense and for some too serious.

Black women of my time, my age, simply were not stepping out and claiming the professional life as comfortable. I enjoyed the challenge of the job, thrived in the fray. While I enjoyed my weekends, I looked forward to getting back to the job to go at it another way. Instead of saying how much I simply liked working and being at the helm, I spoke instead of the issues in the hopes of involving others.

Without ever saying it, I sought the deference that had been given to my uncles and other men who worked long hours, smoked horrid-smelling cigars and had their dinner waiting for them when they got home. I expected—longed for—them to see the connection between what I was doing and the crusades and sacrifices of other strong black women. I wanted them to appreciate my giving back to the community in a significant way.

Luckily for me, I found forums in women's groups. At the urging of my colleague Patricia Carey (no relation to the then-governor), I took a leadership role in the Association of Black Women in Higher Education. Without regard to rank, we came together over what we had in common as black women, namely, the need to confront efforts to marginalize our achievements. I also received a call from Meg Armstrong, executive director of Women Executives in State Government, inviting me to join this group made up of women executives in elected state offices or serving as governor appointees. The focus was networking, support and bolstering our staying power. They were clear about wanting to be at the top, enjoying the heady rush of power. They were less clear about the importance of being an advocate to make sure that those that followed had access to opportunities. This was frustrating for me and kept me off to the side. Yet I stayed with the group, getting from it what I could and ultimately being awarded the group's "Breaking the Glass Ceiling Award."

The bottom line was that we would not achieve success

in the women's movement until we came together around the issues of inequities for all women of color, especially poor women. This would mean dealing with issues on a national and international basis.

We strengthened links to professional associations, Washington lobbyists, college presidents, financial aid officers, legislative assistants, the governor's office, community groups and national advocates. Our actions were meant to get us a seat at the table so we could promote access to higher education for all eligible students. Our relationship with the state Education Department was cool, on the verge of a feud, as the people there felt we were encroaching on their power base. This was problematic because of the joint and overlapping responsibilities of the agencies. I would describe our position as HESC being like David grappling with Goliath in the form of the state Education Department. We didn't back down often. I viewed my task as not letting the agency be captive of any other entity. We had to stay focused on delivering financial aid, providing information and promoting access to financial aid for all eligible students.

It was important for me to define my role and personal responsibility for leadership. I did not want to let external and internal forces pigeonhole me to the point of inaction. I had to keep going, empowering people around me and, in turn, empowering the agency.

Often, I thought of my Uncle Matt's words: "Are they teaching you to think?" I wanted to give people information to help them think things through, to force issues to a dialogue. I was as optimistic as my uncle in believing that using information to think things through meant you'd been more than schooled, you'd been educated.

Were my uncle still alive I would add, "How you use the information is determined in part by how you have been schooled." From my perspective, many people had not been schooled to value diversity or sense a moral imperative to be fair and relate to the realities of the human condition. I knew as well that if progress was not made in giving more people of color access to opportunities, people of color would be picked out of the line as the problem.

MILE 21

Rest is as important as running. It allows me to push forward, renewed and ready for the challenge. I listen to my body. If it tells me not to run, I rest. I also listen to my spirit. It needs the boost I get from running. My spirit is renewed when my feet carry me forward into the wind.

Twice a month I headed my car from Albany to Newark to spend the day with Aunt Jean. She lived in a senior citizens home off Broad Street on the second floor and filled her life with domestic activities. It felt good to be in her presence. She had a schedule of chores for the day. There would be two weeks of shopping, bills to pay, correspondence to catch up on and, on occasion, a visit with her physician or podiatrist. Since 1978, this had been our routine.

I loved being in her small apartment, sensing the aloneness she wore like a warm blanket, and hearing for the first time wonderful stories of her life. I learned how she had worked for various families and had spent years with one family, to the point that they became her extended family. The letters she dictated to me would most often be to this white family. She spoke of studying books on French furniture and how she had decided on each piece to buy. She had waited until she was 37 to marry my Uncle Sam, bringing her furniture to the marriage.

We had laughed until we cried at her stories of growing up on a farm and not wanting any of the animals (she saw them as her pets) slaughtered for meals. There was a tinge of sadness in her voice when she spoke of how her mother had been jealous of her father's open affection for her as his favorite. I heard, too, how she defined what "proper" ladies do: a lone woman does not board an elevator with a strange man nor does she show too much of her legs and arms in public. In her mind, one should always address a married woman as "Mrs." not "Ms." I was surprised to hear her say she regarded widows as still married and expected to be treated by men as such.

My uncle had been dead for close to ten years, yet some of his clothes were still in her closet. She spoke to his picture on the bureau.

Her pride would not permit her to take money from me. After the money she had put away was gone, she arranged for me to sell her parents' house in New Jersey. When that money ran out, we worked out an arrangement where I bought her furniture from her, a piece or two at a time. When she needed money for a television, I said, "Here's $300, and now I 'own' the two needlepoint chairs." They remained with her but were designated as mine. This went on for years. I felt her life, her breath in those possessions. She enjoyed these items as one does a rose or a fine glass of wine. They were for her to savor and to give peace to others in her company. She liked beautiful things, and she was beautiful inside in her kindness and caring for people.

As a young girl I had seen my Aunt Jean as judgmental, concerned too much with how I looked. I realized in my visits that what she was looking for was for my exterior presentation to match what she saw in me.

Our days together ended with dinner. I could not help but miss my uncle and our meals together. I thanked him by spending time with Aunt Jean, well aware that the visits were equally important for me. The visits reminded me of what I grew up with, how fortunate I was to have the family I did. They lifted my spirits.

MILE 22

Mile 22 is a challenge. You need a base of strength, strength that only can be built up over time. You need mileage. You need training. Without these, you are at risk of hitting the wall.

In 1985, I maintained a heavy schedule of TV interviews, press conferences and speaking engagements at more than 60 events. My goal was to engage diverse groups in issues of equality and help them realize how much was at stake if people were not given access to higher education.

In January, I was in Buffalo being interviewed by WKBW-TV to promote Financial Aid Awareness Week. That same month I visited several high schools to demonstrate our financial aid estimating system. In February I was a panelist for a Black and Puerto Rican Legislative Caucus meeting. In March, I testified before the Congressional Black Caucus Braintrust and held a meeting of the committee of 21 college presidents. Later in March I testified at a Senate hearing on the impact of the proposed FY'86 budget on higher education in New York. In April, I held a press conference on consumer issues related to financial aid. In May, I testified on the 1986 federal budget before the Labor, Health and Human Services, Education and Related Appropriations Subcommittee of the Senate Appropriations Committee in Washington, D.C. And I was graduation speaker at Touro College of General Studies. In June, I made a presentation at a meeting of the American Council on Education's National Identification Program of Women in Higher Education. In July, I testified again in Washington, D.C. Skipping August, in September, I judged the New York Statewide Essay Competition. In October, I was keynote speaker for the annual award luncheon of the New York Human Rights Commission in Syracuse, New York. In November, I was a presenter at the New York State Financial Aid Administrators Association meeting. And in December, I made a presentation to the Regents Committee on Higher and Professional Education in Albany.

My mother enjoyed my press clippings. To her and other members of my family, the depth of my participation came through when there was some media account. Yet, I wanted them to understand that it was important not to equate my visibility on the issues as progress. While I was moving ahead far too many were hitting the wall. There was slippage in access to higher education in New York as more and more low-income students were having to rely on loans to complete their financial aid package. Furthermore, many were not being prepared before they went on to college.

My experience with financial aid gave my own family greater access, even though it had nothing to do with my programs. My mother, now a full-time student, relied on the information she got from HESC and the advice she received from Charles Treadwell of the agency's research and information division. My sister, Jean, became quite able not only in estimating resources for her children but in advising other young people in the community. I knew from the experience in my family, that when one member of the family is given a chance, others benefit. My experiences were having a second-generation impact.

My own children benefited as well, not only from the information I was able to share but with the risks I was taking. Jane graduated cum laude from the University of California, Davis, and went on to the University of Michigan Law School, with an emphasis on international law. At only 21, she had graduated and was looking to join a law firm in New York City. Tom Jr. had graduated from Sonoma and begun teaching music in northern California.

On a personal level they both struggled in the aftermath of the divorce. They expected an explanation from their father, his version of the failed marriage. "He was a great father, but not a great divorced dad," they said. They were united in being critical of both their parents for not dealing with the impact on them of moving from town to town. Nor were they pleased that both of us continued to move from place to place in our separate lives.

I was still getting started on what I viewed as my mission of insuring access at a time when some of my friends were looking at hanging it up as they too were close to 50. The first was the proclamation of my friend Betty as she made a dramatic toast in celebration of her 50th birthday in 1986. "It's all downhill after 50," she exclaimed as she raised her glass. She was like a bird leaving the challenge of the skies to peck at the crumbs on the ground. I couldn't relate, as I felt ready to fly straighter, steadier and higher than I ever had before. I wanted to soar. No crumbs for me.

I thought of a conversation she and I had after reading an article by Terry McMillan in the "Hers" column of *The New York Times*, "Two Mr. Wrongs." To some of my friends, the article deftly and not too subtly trashed black men as abdicating their responsibilities. "I identify with it 100 percent," Betty said, adding that she felt what had been described about black men included all the men in our lives—sons, brothers and fathers—not just lovers and husbands. What's more, she said, white men were falling into this pattern.

Most black women, she went on, are tired of giving, giving, giving, giving. "We are tired of being put down and getting our butts kicked. It is time for us to stop making excuses, stop being supportive and start kicking butt ourselves," she said, on a roll. "I hope the young women of today don't waste a lot of their time, energy and money on male/female relationships unless the couple is committed to each other and dedicated to the social, emotional and financial well-being of each other."

I tried to put the two conversations together, the "it's all downhill at 50" and the "let's start kicking black men's butts." I realized I hadn't focused on either of her points. I was feeling strong, ready to move on as I neared 50. I had not, to my thinking, let a relationship with a man constrain me or suppress my ambition. Sure, I'd been intimidated, diminished by negative comments from men who made more of the white standards of beauty. And sure, in my relationship with Tom, I had let his wishes be at the center. But he hadn't gotten in my way. And while I knew of women who had mothers who had been walked on like doormats by men, many other black women were like my grandmother. She let my grandfather get away with some stuff, but she walked tall, made do and defied him as often as she seemed to comply. And I could not imagine a man convincing my mother that there was something she could not accomplish. She had shown my father the door, before it was commonplace to do so. And I saw my Aunt Jean achieve what she wanted in the space that was home for her and my uncle. With the exception of a desk she identified as his desk, the apartment was as feminine as one could imagine. I saw in my Aunt Carolyn, my father's only sister and the youngest, a woman who, while not invited to join her brothers in their business, started her own series of businesses. Plus, she earned undergraduate and graduate degrees. My sister, Jean, had a way of seeming to defer to her husband, Jake, while still leading. She would call on Jake to make a decision to resolve an issue, yet it was clear she had steered the decision in a certain direction beforehand. Priding herself for having maintained a sound marriage, she viewed it as an achievement against which my accomplishments paled.

The women I knew from my childhood were ageless, independent, doing what they wanted and needed to do with or in spite of men. I thought of the black women, who like me, had worked to balance family and professional lives. Some had been in rocky relationships, to put it mildly, and no longer wanted to raise men anymore. They wanted equal time and needed stroking, too. If a relationship couldn't be built on reciprocity, they didn't want it. Most often we didn't want to spend the rest of our lives unhappy with men; we could be unhappy alone. In fact, it could be more lonely when you were with someone than when you were not, if your expectations were different. We wanted to move ahead and not be bogged down by the insecurities, perceived inadequacies and paranoia of our men. By and large, we had put men on notice, not by taking them on but rather by doing what we had to do remaining strong and beautiful in spirit.

Terry McMillan represented the generation of women behind me. At the time of her column, white women were entering the professions and the labor force in great numbers. Young black men who were regarded as the cream of the crop were not falling in love with the cream of the crop black women, but were in some cases attracted to white women. And all too often, black women entered relationships where their men tried to tame them. Unlike in my growing up days, young black women were saying, "We can be happy single," or in an interracial or same-sex relationship.

Despite our history and bravado, black women of my generation spent our times together talking about our children or good-humoredly trashing our men or the shape of our bodies. I folded over in laughter as the women friends who gathered most often at Betty's talked about a future of sagging breasts, dragging butts and flab, flab, flab.

There was Betty's "better than sex" chocolate cake and coffee while we mulled over the inevitable. And they turned to me at some point and remarked: "Dee's gonna kill herself yet, riding her new Raleigh bike down Second Avenue, roller-skating in the Village and ice skating in Albany. Girl, you had better get a grip. You can't stop that belly roll from going south." I would not separate myself from my friends by telling them I wanted more. I wanted economic independence and I wanted to leave a legacy.

MILE 23

"I'M 50 AND GOING THE DISTANCE"
I pull the shirt bearing those words over my head. What's 50 anyway? What's 50 on this cool fall day as I get ready to run? What's 50 when I am here to run my first marathon? I'm 50 and going the distance. It's my recital and the music is me.

Three months after Betty's birthday, I fell and broke my ankle ice skating in Albany. I'd been wanting to take charge. "I can carry my own bags, thank you very much" was my approach to everything. And there I was, unable to do the simplest of tasks. Betty regarded my broken ankle and wounded spirit as preparation for the inevitable downhill slide into old age. Fortunately, her resignation on my behalf was countered by my physical therapist who advised that if I followed instructions, I would be able to tackle anything I wanted to do. I responded, "I want to run the New York City Marathon."

Two months after my cast came off, I began training. I had never run more than three miles before. Indeed it had been 36 years since I had run in junior high school competively. My New Year's resolution was to stabilize my health. I confided to Ted that I would use training for the marathon as the means. "Can't you just get healthy without having to go to the extreme of a marathon?" he asked with his eyebrows raised.

But for me, it was all or nothing. My decision to go for the marathon meant I'd be out there achieving all I was capable of achieving. It would be a statement that I was taking charge of my life. I'd do it.

I began slowly, mixing walking and running and taking excursions to the park to observe other runners. I was surprised by the number of people out there, running alone, in pairs or in groups. They had been there before, but I hadn't really noticed them. By the end of the first month, I had settled

on a late evening run around campus of the State University
of New York in Albany. I was running, mimicking the style of
other runners, keeping my arms low, maintaining a steady
pace, holding my hips tucked in and my shoulders relaxed.

I visualized going the distance, as I thought of the train
engine in the children's book, *The Little Engine That Could*,
coaching myself with the slightly grander approach: "I know I
can, I know I can, I know I can." I trained by time, not by distance. I began with 20 minutes, extending the time gradually
to 30, then 40 minutes. By the end of three weeks, I was running 40 minutes a day, five days a week, at a very slow steady
pace. My legs felt very heavy, but I was not hurting.

I purchased a book on runners' injuries to know what to
look for and avoid the problems that sidelined so many people.
Convinced of my need to learn more about running from runners, I joined the New York Road Runners Club. I developed
friendships based on discussions about recovering from
injuries, strategies for racing and planning for the marathon.

Truly competitive runners don't share all their secrets, I
found. They tend to hold back something. And whatever you
do learn you have to spin for your own purposes. For example, slowing down to a walk has never worked to keep me
going. When I'm tired, I have to keep running, reducing my
pace, but not falling back to a walk.

Five weeks after I began my training, I ran my first race. I
trudged in close to last to finish a 5K in 37 minutes. But I finished. That race tipped me off about how runners view each
other's ages. A 45-year-old woman smiled broadly as she told
me about the advantage she had in moving into the 45-to-50
age category by having a birthday the week before. The runners all peered at each others' racing bibs to determine ages
and who they had to beat. I never heard a runner say to another runner, "You look good for your age." Running is about feeling good for your age and being blessed to be able to go the
distance.

After that race, I began to pace runs to cover a specific
number of miles a day. In training for a marathon, if your

physical stamina allows only three miles that day, fine. Three miles it is, for that day. But the goal is still 26.2 miles. Each day I pushed myself to go farther. By June, I had worked my way up to five to six miles a day and 30 to 35 miles a week. I scheduled long runs around New York's Central Park on Sundays. My days became defined in terms of having had a good run or a bad run. The challenge was consuming. Alternately, I experienced the runner's high—a glorious feeling of invincibility— or great humility when I pushed on through the rain or through my aches and pains.

I scheduled appointments for running on my calendar and kept them without fail. Most often I had to run in the evening, yet I preferred the morning runs. Running was about maintaining momentum. So was my work. I handled the stress of my Board, legislators, the governor's office, community activists, and university and college presidents. The agency had set a pace and raised new expectations. I brought running; being strong was a skill I found myself bringing to leadership.

I looked to make good decisions based on information about everything from running shoes and health food supplements to cross training. I learned to trust only running-shoe clerks who were experienced runners.

When my enthusiasm for running waned, I played mind games. Most often, I was a slave getting away from "massa" to freedom. Or I imagined my father ahead and his saying: "Go, baby. Look at you go." And I could always motivate myself by phoning either of my children. They could hear me dragging and say, "Did you run today?" or "Go for your run, Mom."

I improved my speed training, running the 5K in New York City in 24 minutes and the Freihofer 10K in Albany in 49.2 minutes. I took the stairs, sought out hills and increased my mileage to as much as 40 miles a week. I felt strong as I approached the first real test in July, the New York City Hispanic Half Marathon, which I completed in 2 hours and 16 minutes. It was grueling. I suddenly understood the depth of the challenge of going the distance of the whole marathon. I appreciated how far I had come. And yet how I still had far to go to run 26.2 miles. I began to add more speed runs to my schedule.

Later that summer I discovered running camp. Among the brochures at the New York Running Club was one on the Craftsbury Running Camp in Craftsbury, Vermont. I lost no time before applying, and in early August I found myself in "runners' heaven." There were no worries about turning people off in talking about your aches, pains and mileage. You could, in this oasis high in the lush hills of Vermont, wrap yourself in running from early morning until you put your head down at night. There were no phones, television, *Bibles*, keys or private baths in our comfortable, sparse barracks. There were magazines on running, fitness and diet in the public space. While we reveled in our running stories, we privately worried about fellow campers who were almost out of control. One was intent on running 100 miles in one week. She had to be returned to the camp by a tourist one day after she got lost in the Vermont hills. She also would, with only the slightest urging, join you for a turn after completing her own long run. At the end of the two weeks, we equipped her with a miner's cap with a lamp for night running. I wondered if I was seeing my future in her. In time would I be out of control with my running?

By September, I had instructed my friends not to call me after 9:30 p.m.

Throughout August, September and October I ran five to six days a week. I included speed and hill work. And I cross-trained, alternating cycling with the Stairmaster. I extended my long runs every other week. By late September I ran my longest run, 20 miles.

Some friends were encouraging, others questioning. A woman associate expressed her concern that my running was a neurotic denial of my age. Another acquaintance observed that my relationships came second to my running. Yet I was conscious of achieving a balance, of feeling less vulnerable and less like a victim of a failed marriage. I felt intact, and pushing on bolstered my sense of personal achievement.

In daily runs, I pressed on through rain and exhaustion by thinking about the feeling of pride and joy I had when on a sunny day in Newark, at the age of 11, I marched in my freshly starched and ironed gym uniform in the parade of young athletes down the hill toward the running track. I remembered my intense sense of accomplishment as the team achieved first place.

I was rediscovering physical discipline and nurturing my inner strength with each step. This resiliency allowed me to feel peace. It was okay to be alone. I was defining who I was and determining how I'd do in a very different challenge.

My friends and family voiced their concern with what they called "Dolores' obsession." My mother worried about my getting hurt. One friend went so far as to say, "Perhaps the running will calm you down and help you not be as crazy as the other achieving, self-absorbed older women I know." I refused to be self-conscious as I reflected on the comments of others. I had changed in body tone and in attitude. I was ready.

As November approached and marathon day grew closer, I grew bold in my declaration to go the distance. I planned a post-marathon party at my New York City apartment and invited family, friends and colleagues to celebrate. I kept myself fired up with the desire to defy the myth that an African American woman at my age wouldn't be poised for the challenge. My running would honor my ancestors. The November event overshadowed other days and activities of consequence. I was focused in my intentions: to do it, run strong and smart.

The night before, I feasted on pasta and told my family and friends how I had lined up with thousands of people in Central Park to get the marathon application when it came out. Doing so increased my chances for acceptance. I handled all the details myself, finally putting all of those energies that went into doing things for other people into doing something for myself. "I am woman, I am strong," I hummed over and over to myself.

Marathon day began at 4:45 a.m., when I got up early to board the bus at the New York City Public Library at Fifth Avenue and 42nd. The buses took me and thousands of others, speaking seemingly every language on Earth, to the staging area at Staten Island. Before the 10:30 a.m. start, runners from around the world waited in tents grouped by friendship or language.   I found a spot in the middle of a tent and tried to stretch some and then rest. I was much too excited to be still. I walked to the water tables to fill up and back to the toilets to relieve myself.

The press of people made it impossible to find my space once I gave it up. But it felt like a community, full of a calm and quiet excitement as volunteers encouraged and helped the runners prepare themselves. Amidst the blur of runners, I moved to the starting line to cross the Verrazano Narrows Bridge. The gun must have cracked because the runners shuffled out to find their space and pace. I felt the rush, the exhilaration as the helicopter hovered overhead. I was in it.

The marathon took me through every borough in New York City, past huge crowds, music and words of encouragement. The music was diverse and spirited: jazz, salsa, polka, gospel. The noise of clapping, cheering and calling out of race numbers was piercing and encouraging.

My shirt read, "I AM 50 AND GOING THE DISTANCE." The crowd responded. "I don't believe it." "Looking good, sister." "Way to go!"   I set no time to finish, just wanting to finish comfortably and enjoy the distance.

I was feeling my legs and arms and the weight of pulling my body up and down with each comfortable stride.   The lessons of my training ran through my head: Start slow and strong, build to a comfortable pace, keep moving, even as you stop for water at every stop. Remember, much of what you do is attitude, spirit and confidence.   One foot, then another.

As I approached Harlem, there were more screams of encouragement and hand slapping. My running meant "we as blacks" were going the distance. People were visibly proud and expressing disbelief at my announced age. "Sister, you don't have to tell nobody." "You look better than my old lady and she's 25." And so often, "God bless you." My sister, brother-in-law and mother were at mile 20, all smiles.

I moved ahead to Central Park, looking forward to the finish. My children would be there to cheer me through. The crowds at Central Park were enormous. It had been over two hours since the winners had passed through, yet people remained cheering us on as winners, too.

Turning in facing the finish line, I quickened my pace, pumped my arms, smiled and crossed the line in 4 hours and 42 minutes. I'd done it.

MILE 24

I get to and through my paces by reading, observing and talking each race through ahead of time. It's part of what must be done to get through. The race is life to be lived and experienced.

The steps I had taken were mine. No one could claim them or deny them or doubt that I had determined my own direction. In a stereotypical way, my running a physical marathon was more believable than the reality of my having achieved a personal best as president of the New York State Higher Education Services Corporation (HESC). It was real. The physical feat of completing 26.2 miles of running communicated more than the steps I had taken to achieve success in my career. I was not happy with this observation.

I was credited with having put together a top-notch team but was thought by some to be the cheerleader, not the captain. The guys on the team led and played ball, they thought. So be it. I would continue running marathons. And I would continue coaching, leading and being a member of the team. And I would be clear about what I'd achieved out of my running shoes. As I entered my seventh year as president of HESC, Governor Mario Cuomo invited members of his cabinet to share with him what each of us would like to see as our legacy. I was eager to respond:

> As I thought about what I would like my legacy to be I was reminded of the challenge to remember who we are and where our roots lie. In helping others within the family of New York, we all gain.... In all that I have done, I have always worked to keep the student clearly in mind. Keeping the student clearly in focus also helps me recognize what is at stake: maintaining New York's strength through diversity and actualizing its commitment to equity. As I look back over the years I have served as president of HESC, I find that the range of New Yorkers receiving

financial aid is as broad as the population itself.
Regardless of where people come from—a housing project
in the Bronx, a suburb outside Buffalo or a farm in Broome
County—and regardless of whether they are low income,
middle income or high income they can have trouble paying for college.

From my experience, I know and understand a basic
truth: that while the neediest still need help, paying for
college has become a problem for all of us. However, we
must not forget that the neediest continue to be, by and
large, our black and Hispanic students, who for too long
have been disadvantaged by lack of opportunities.

In my opinion more must be done on the issue of
access. We must do more than merely acknowledge the
underrepresentation of racially and linguistically different
students on college campuses. We have an obligation to
take a more proactive stance by asking ourselves challenging questions such as:

Have we worked to promote access today?

On a results basis, what have we achieved?

Have we helped each other achieve common goals?

What have we been doing in the short and long term to
increase minority access, retention, graduation and work-
place opportunities?

We also have to examine these questions on a personal
basis by asking ourselves:

Do we see the despair?

Do we care?

Do we in a real sense, remember who we are?

Are we as compassionate as we should be or as we pur-
port to be?

I would like my legacy to be that I asked and tried to
answer the right questions.

When I raised the question in the legacy statement to
Governor Cuomo—"Do we see the despair?"—I realized what
he might see would be different from my experience. Among
my black colleagues in higher education there was indeed
despair and disappointment. For the most part we were iso-
lated, yet intent on documenting our contribution in teaching,

research and administration. We shared our stories in meetings such as the American Educational Research Association's "Special Interest Group: Research Focus on Black Education." Often we were perceived as less qualified, less valuable and less acceptable than our white peers. Our credentials and contributions were not believed. The pattern of selecting a few blacks and regarding them as exceptional while disregarding so many others was apparent, especially as conference planners looked for the black stars.

You had to get a hook, a gimmick, quite often to gain attention. As my racing and marathoning continued, they became a tag associated with me. It was an opener for a conversation, especially the fact that I'd run my first marathon at age 50.

Most often I wanted to keep my colleagues in touch with the despair, the kind of despair that had gripped my friend James Deslonde, when the gate to tenure had been closed to him at Stanford. He moved on, made a life for himself, yet he was lost to the world of academe. The Stanford experience was devastating for him. Jim had gone to work for a research firm in the Palo Alto area. The Christmas after I completed my second marathon, Jim sent me some red roses and called a week later. We spoke of the setbacks caused by not having mentors and being discouraged by subtle and not-so-subtle messages. We lost touch for a few months. I was filled with grief when in 1988 I learned of his early death.

So much of what we all do is to collect items to share, to be good company for someone who matters. When a friend dies, you think of how the time taken up in your daily struggle deprived you of a good conversation or the time to write a letter. Jim had not turned 50.

A few months later, Betty died as well. She had an adverse reaction to a medical treatment, developed respiratory problems and went quickly. She had not reached 55.

I saw and tried to hide my grief, looking at Betty's weakness. Her breathing was labored, her words forced. She gasped as she immediately reached for oxygen. Each word was difficult and there were pauses as she sought more oxygen. She seemed to have atrophied from the neck down, fighting, yet failing, and needing the nourishment of concern. Would she win? What was the prognosis? I felt her losing, not dying.   I recalled with her how during her pregnancy she couldn't shampoo her hair. She had put on so much weight it was difficult for her to lean over the bowl to rinse and work her hair. I came over to do it. We spoke of her babysitting Tom Jr. and his rolling off the bed—and how that of course was the reason for all Tommy's problems. She coughed through laughter, not moving from the chair as if the fellowship of the moment would be altered if she went to the bathroom or requested to be shifted.

I should have seen the signs of her dying—I missed them—yet there they were. God, they were there on that last day as she spoke of the loss her son would feel when she was gone. "He's not prepared. Who will look out for him?" She all but asked me to make a commitment to be in charge of him. I felt, without her saying, that she would watch out for Tommy and Jane, if the situation were reversed. It felt right just to listen. I can't recall my response.

Her chest heaved and her eyes filled with the plea. She talked and then wept as she spoke of death, and in the next breath, talked easily of managing to survive. As I listened and read her prescription, I blamed both her and her physician for what was happening.

Did I hear her rasp when she said the doctor had continued her on steroids despite the fact she was allergic to steroids and that she was being weaned from them? Did she also say again that this physician had helped her secure early disability retirement because of the illness that racked her body?   And that the disability payment would keep her going? Is this madness? How deep is the sickness? Where did she find this warped formula for survival?

I suspected some deal with Faust. I brought myself back from my mental tirades to her room, her plans, expectations and her condition. I was responsible, I felt, for the new strength and hope she seemed to have. I knew she would share the news of my visit and my promise to return again.

Within a week she returned to the hospital. When I visited she greeted me as if she had been abandoned by others, sharing how close friends were deceiving her. I should have said yes instead of thinking about my Manhattan appointment when she asked me to visit again. It was not enough that I'd visited twice that month; I was passing by another opportunity with a promise to return in a week. She nodded. I recognized her hope that it would happen, yet she had experienced my pattern of promises. I wrote the following in my journal:

> When a friend dies, I think most often of what we expect of each other and what I can continue to do, as if I am in that friend's company still. I think of the phone calls and dates I missed as I dealt with matters of consequence. I keep in mind that my friends know and accept me as I am. They accept and respect my involvement, my passion and willingness to try to make a difference. Their deaths remind me of my mortality. Jim and Betty join others who I think about on my daily runs, listening to my breath and steps, while keeping track of where I'm going.

MILE 25

Practice your breathing. Breathe in for three counts and out for three counts. Listen to each breath. Life is breath, breath is action. You're breathing, acting and staying in touch with yourself. Your strength comes from this rhythm of your life.

It was Clift Wharton, chancellor of the New York State University System, who advised me, "If you're really serious about a college presidency, take a number two or three position in academic affairs to strengthen your academic credentials, preferably at a research institution." There was a tug inside me telling me to get out of state government after having been president of HESC for almost eight years and being described as the old timer in a state agency leadership position. These agency jobs are political, and if you're around too long, someone will find a way to get you out.

Not long after my meeting with Clift, I saw an announcement for the position of associate provost and associate vice president for academic affairs, with responsibility for minority affairs, at the University of Minnesota. The job was at the senior staff level, with faculty rank and tenure status and major responsibilities in providing leadership and direction for 52 programs in the entire university system. The job also provided for increased responsibilities beyond minority affairs after initial organization of the office.

After a national search, the university selected me for the position.

In May 1988, I resigned as president of the New York State Higher Education Services Corporation. It had been a defining period for me. I was confident about my role as an advocate and leader, and Governor Cuomo affirmed my contribution in a letter saying he was sorry to receive my resignation:

You have been an innovative advocate for improved access to higher education, particularly for women and minorities, and you have personally served as an extraordinary role model for the young people of our State. Your efforts to bring the benefits of expanded student financial assistance to those most in need and your championing of innovative approaches such as Liberty Scholarships have produced a legacy of which you should be rightly proud. I wish you every possible success as you return to the academic community.
Sincerely, Mario

When I began mentally readying myself for the move, I was struck with how accustomed to being alone. I was. Handling personal changes, my empty nest, paying college costs for my children, relocating frequently, transitions in the lives of family and friends, I now preferred running alone. The move to Minnesota would be my first move alone without proximity to family. I'd have to establish myself in a job and make new friends.

My mother viewed the relocation as a positive step. She liked the idea of my not having the top job and the buck stopping at my desk. She envisioned me winding down.

That summer before I left for Minnesota, I dedicated an address to her at Skidmore College on the occasion of receiving my second honorary degree. My address, titled "Is a Chance Too Much to Ask For? Is a Chance Too Much to Give?" spoke to the chances I had been given and what I saw as my responsibility to give others a chance.

From the stage I looked at my mother and Jane in the audience. I knew my mother would appreciate my heralding her as the first black female to pass the civil service exam for telephone operator in New Jersey, a lifelong learner for more than 20 years and, in 1988 at the age of 70, a full-time student at Union College in New Jersey. She stood proud and I got to salute her in front of everyone.

The address at Skidmore was my last presentation as president of the New York State Higher Education Services

Corporation. I appealed to the graduates:

> Our challenge is to create a deepening human sensitiv-
> ity, a broadening of our compassion for one another and a
> strengthening of our awareness of issues that confront us
> in a complex multicultural society. The major social prob-
> lems of crime and violence, drug abuse, child and spouse
> abuse, chronic welfare dependency, high unemployment,
> children failing to learn in school, elitism in higher educa-
> tion, as well as racial tensions on college campuses, will
> continue to plague our society if you, we, individually and
> collectively, fail to fulfill our potential to make a differ-
> ence.
>
> Ask of yourself and others: Is a chance too much to ask
> for? Is a chance too much to give? Remember, today, oth-
> ers equally eager, motivated, who for reasons of societal
> indifference, racism, sexism or poverty, didn't have a
> chance.   Recall how indifference and benign neglect
> destroy self-esteem. Carry with you the responsibility to
> ensure that those who come after you and share the desire
> for education that you have, have the opportunity to reach
> their goals too. And consider also how in undertaking a
> social responsibility you unlock the secret of fulfilling
> your potential as an educator, lawyer, parent, dancer,
> musician or marathon runner.
>
> I urge you to continue to believe in yourself and in the
> hope you represent to others. If you do, no aspiration will
> be too great and goal unreachable.

I drove directly from Skidmore in Saratoga Springs, New
York, to Newark to visit Aunt Jean.   I felt without her saying
how much hope I represented to her. When others did not
come because of their schedules or her reluctance to see them,
she knew I would travel to be with her and take care of her.
Having fallen a month ago, she was now managing alone from
her wheelchair in her small two-bedroom apartment.

When I arrived, I found her seated in her wheelchair. I
smelled urine. She confessed she was unable to navigate to the
bathroom or to her bed. She had slept in her wheelchair and
was sipping barely enough water to cover her thirst, so as not

to wet even more. We conspired together how we might get past this bad time. Neither of us wanted to fail, as we knew full well the hope we represented to each other. I was learning from her how to be alone, to go the distance.

After cleaning her and helping her get into her bed, I sat and talked to her about better times. We read the birthday cards she had received from my Uncle Sam over the years. Despite his busy days, he had found time to purchase these cards, some with lace and all protected by my aunt with layers of wax paper. She listened as I told her again of my plans to move again, this time to Minnesota. She agreed with my mother that it was time for me to move on to a less stressful position.

She brightened as I told her how I had arranged to teach a contract course at Baruch College, CUNY, which meant I would keep my apartment in New York City and be on the East Coast every other week to monitor her situation. We knew that the move meant that we would have to accelerate our finding an acceptable home for her.

By the end of the summer, we had located a new nursing home in South Orange, New Jersey, and agreed that I would keep the furniture in New York and continue to pay expenses as I had for the past 10 years. I was committed both to moving ahead and being there, racing and pacing back and forth, buoyed by my energy, aware of giving back.

Ted Jackson helped me with the move to Minneapolis, as he'd helped me move to my apartment in Albany. He had encouraged me to return to my tenured position as professor at Brooklyn College, yet he supported my choice and new direction.

Claremont was a postage stamp compared with the vastness of the University of Minnesota, where armies of students—few of color—moved back and forth. As the university's first black female administrator in the newly created position of associate vice president and associate provost of academic affairs, I was meant to hit the ground running and address longstanding concerns of equity and access for minorities. As in running, I knew I had to have a plan, assert my goals, maintain a pace and motivate others to get on with what needed to be done.

We developed a blueprint for action to guide diversity initiatives on the four campuses. The plan required departments and schools to set goals and design strategies for recruitment and faculty and staff development on the retention of students of color. The budget for the program permitted me to provide incentive grants for departments and colleges that developed credible plans. I initiated the first university-wide education fest, which invited precollege students from all over the state to Duluth to interact with faculty, learn of financial aid opportunities and participate in cultural activities that celebrated diversity. Dollars were also provided to support the hiring of minorities and operate summer bridge programs.

"The job is not 10K, it is a marathon," was what I told Dennis Cabral as I implored him to join me in Minnesota as director of precollege programs. Dennis was familiar with my working style. He knew I wouldn't be daunted by coming into the job from the outside. We counted on each other, and six months after my arrival in Minnesota, Dennis and his wife, Elke, joined me.

As I had in Albany, I found friends and associates who too were runners. Bobbi and Alan Isaacman and I would meet for long runs around Lake Calhoun. We'd maintain an even clip for seven to eight miles conversing as expatriates from New York City. "This place is not really a city, it's just a big town." We went on and on about the diversion running provided and how runners have a way of using analogies from running in all they do. Bobbi worked providing legal services for the poor, and Alan, professor in African Studies, headed the MacArthur Peace and International Studies Program, with the goal of increasing the number of minorities in doctoral programs. We recognized in each other that our "1960s commitment" had grown stronger with discipline. While we joked about the "niceness" of Minnesota, we were comfortable both with it and the New York "toughness" we could bring to people's reluctance to "do the right thing" or, even worse, to understand. For us, the revolution continued.

I stayed in the Lake Calhoun area, moving from an apartment to a house. I wanted my house in Minneapolis to be a place my children might see as their family home. The house at 3621 S. Bryant had a special feel. Sandwiched between two multi-level apartment buildings, it had a deep front porch, a full backyard and an unattached garage. It was constructed with a simplicity in accord with my spirit: hardwood floors and wood warm trim, three rooms upstairs and three rooms down. In buying the house, I made my first big purchase as a single woman in a place where many women seemed to be redefining their lives.

I was taken by the kindness of a group of women runners who approached me to warn me of the dangers of running alone in secluded areas. There had been a rape recently of a lone runner. "Look for other runners, wear a whistle and report anything that looks strange or menacing," one told me before sharing the times of their early morning runs. Most often I would be out by 5:45 a.m. and back before 7 a.m. On some cold Minnesota mornings, I brushed ice from my lashes and made the first prints in deep snow. I could not wait for Minnesota's "three months of warmth." I had to keep moving and stay strong.

Given the difficulty of white women in dealing with sexism at the university, I knew that someone would try to marginalize my impact by narrowly defining my role as "chief of diversity" or "head Negro in charge of making it look good." I pre-empted an attack by talking with my colleagues on the whole range of issues in academic affairs. I was projecting my voice and point of view as a black woman who was not content to comment on one corner of the mountain, but rather wanted to ascend to a higher view of the range.

I spoke of my restlessness and concern on a campus that professed a liberal tradition, yet had fewer than 1,000 black students in a population of more 35,000. Students told me about faculty members who were not interested in their success. And

I was aware that this was another institution that pitted women against minorities and minorities against each other by limiting the resources for improvement.

I was not stilled by the niceness of Minnesota or its liberal promise. Most often I seemed to be challenging a few white women who expected me to champion their cause as if I were not black as well as female. My strident approach was as difficult for some white women as it was for white men. This happened most often when I asked why minority candidates had been passed over in favor of a white woman.

The converging roles of being an advocate for underrepresented minorities, a mother and a caregiver weighed heavily. I wanted to do more for students. I wanted to give more back. I longed to be a college president and create a model of a university that in all its actions communicated that students of color matter. I also wanted to help my children and be able to fix things for them and listen to them.

Jane told me, "You should have been there when we were children." Tommy spoke of how the move from Evanston happened when he was about to enter a great music program at Evanston High School. I was guilty and felt it! I was guilty of "following my bliss," as the saying goes.

They were on their own, but they kept in touch with sometimes daily calls, Tommy from California and Jane from Chicago.

Tommy had begun to teach music. "Music is my mistress," he always answered when I asked who he was dating. He knew the question meant, "Are you dating any black women?" When Jane was in college, she had invited Tommy to a party with her AKA (Alpha Kappa Alpha) sorority sisters and Tommy embarrassed her by spending the evening dancing with the only white woman she had invited. Tommy could turn it up on both Jane and me by reminding us how in Claremont he'd dated a young black woman who in her "great love" for him chased him home with a gun when he was inattentive. Our reminders of the gun being unloaded made little difference. He also could get to me by making it clear that I had "caused the problem by relocating in white neighborhoods and advocating multiculturalism."

My daily calls with Jane focused most often on her disappointment with the practice of law and the positive diversion she was experiencing in Buddhism. Being an attorney was boring, she said, and it was even more oppressive having to bill hours. It didn't fit her desire to be more creative. A reminder about her student loans led to her lamentation that I didn't understand. Furthermore, my being her mother was part of the problem. As she saw it, I was absorbed in my life's work and would not, as I should, focus on the impact of all my comings and goings on her. I grieved that in all I was doing of "consequence," I could not fix what was wrong for her.

My mother called to urge me to slow down and also to get involved with yet another discrimination case she had against the state of New Jersey. She had been passed over for a position as supervisor for a white woman, after she had come out first on the list. She was fighting to get the pay differential she lost when the job went to the other woman. She also was worried that I ultimately would be stopped in my tracks by an injustice. Racism would claim another casualty. But she also wanted me to take the time for a bus trip with her to the Grand Canyon. "Dolores," she said. "Find time for yourself. You've done enough."

I had not expected the call from the senior home in South Orange advising me that my Aunt Jean was being transferred to another facility in New Jersey. They described her as "difficult to please" and as one who behaved as if she was "too good to fit into the prescribed program." It had done no good to share with the staff how indignant she felt to be bathed by a male orderly or how she might reject food which to her thinking did not represent the right food combination. While she might appear delicate in her taste and voice, Aunt Jean was a strong woman with rules about decorum and what was right. They were treating her as deprived. She consented to the transfer and was moved to South Jersey.

When I visited, I found her expressionless, as if she did

not know me. I talked and searched her face but her eyes showed that she had retreated from me. I should have been the one to find her a new place. Her manner was caused partly by medication, but mostly by her resignation. I felt that I had left her alone to die while I moved ahead. I thought back to our time together in her apartment when she understood my work and the depth of my desire to "like Sam, give something back." The light green walls of the large room grew closer as I sat there with her, still and vacant.

Within a week of that visit she died. She had signed her insurance policy over to a neice, Hestor, from her family, and I arranged a meeting in which Hestor was to sign the policy to pay for the cost of the funeral. Hestor cashed the policy, took the money and left me to pay for the funeral and remaining expenses. I tried but I could not be angry. Aunt Jean had taught me so much and loved me so well.

1989, the year she died, was the same in which I ran three marathons in the 50-to-54 age category: Grandma's in Duluth, the Twin Cities in Minneapolis/St. Paul and the New York City Marathon. I'd done a personal best in Twin Cities, completing the 26.2 miles in 3 hours and 37 minutes.

The marathon race was not over, and I was not running alone.

MILE 25.1

Keep moving. Be distracted by the cheering, the singing and the playing of the musicians. But just keep moving. Visualize your steps, hear your pacing. Imagine you're tapping your toe each time you place your foot. Gotta get through it. Gotta get through it. Feeling good, feeling strong, no problem, no problem. You can do it. Just keep moving, moving ahead.

In 1990, I was nominated and selected to become the first female head of a four-year public university in the state of Illinois. It had been the reference from Peter Drucker that led to my being interviewed for the presidency of Chicago State University, a predominantly black institution of higher education on Chicago's South Side. Peter warned me of how intensely political Chicago would be. At the same time, he said he knew I wouldn't be able to resist a challenge that "most people would have the good sense to turn down."

I knew I wanted a presidency, especially one at an urban university. CSU's undergraduate student profile was very similar to my own background in New Jersey. Students, more women than men, were attending school a mixture of full- and part-time, usually juggling work and family responsibilities. I could understand their exhaustion at the end of the day, their needs for encouragement and support.

But it was not until I actually visited the expansive 167-acre campus of Chicago State University with its 90 percent African American student population that I realized that the job was what I had been preparing all my life to do. As I listened to students, faculty, administrators and university trustees, I heard a real commitment to CSU's success. But they also could have recited (and sometimes did) a litany of problems they perceived: low morale on campus, a poor public image of the university and low student retention.

What was needed, I heard them saying, was a president

who would be a change agent. This leader had to hit the ground running and persevere until CSU glinted and glowed like a polished jewel. I was confident that my base of personal experience and professional work had readied me for the opportunity.

I felt the rush of falling in love with Chicago State University as being on the starting line of an exhilarating marathon. "I can do it," I told myself. I was at the start, and there were 26.2 miles to go.

MILE 25.5

It's risky to do your personal best. Sometimes you push too hard, get away too soon. You refuse to deal with the pain. You dig deep inside yourself. The body is about to rebel but you drive yourself on. There is yet another record to set. Those are dangerous moments.

From the projects in Newark to the president's residence on Longwood Drive in Chicago—what a journey! The twelve-year-old girl in me wanted to run through the 14-room mansion and touch everything. I wanted to share its vastness with my mother and Jean. Its seven bedrooms, six baths, two formal dining rooms, huge living room, sun room, wide elegant staircase, ornate master bedroom and pink marble master bathroom were almost otherworldly, palace-like. How many years before had I spent my homeless nights in the Salvation Army facility? The president's residence was a marvelous setting for Aunt Jean's dining room set, needlepoint chairs and bedroom set. Her spirit blessed each room as I placed her things in my new home.

Ma was thrilled to hear that her daughter was going to live in a "mansion." I loved to tell her all about the room where she would sleep when she visited. But she kept prodding me to describe the symbolic "house" I would create for the students at CSU. I told her that one of my tasks was affirming education as an important and strong tradition in the black community. CSU was more than bricks and mortar, grass and trees, I told her in one of our endless phone calls. It was a place of expectations, a place where dreams could be realized and attained, a place where people who were educationally underserved and academically underprepared could prepare themselves to pursue meaningful and satisfying careers and be productive members of their communities. Ma approved.

Coming to Chicago State University when it had both budget and image problems meant I would be its chief advocate and promoter. Fewer than 20 percent of CSU students completed their degrees in four years. I would need to convince the Board of Governors System, the Illinois Board of Higher Education and the Illinois Legislature that CSU deserved increased resources. I had to improve the way people on the inside and the outside viewed CSU.

"What will Dennis do as you move on to Chicago?" my mother asked me. Indeed, I invited Dennis to lunch to share my news. He listened, aware of the opportunities for me and what my news could mean to him. Only a year before, I had convinced him to come to Minnesota, reassuring him and his wife, Elke, that it would be a good move. But Dennis was aware of my restlessness on a campus where there were few black students. He knew I was in a situation where I couldn't maintain the momentum I had built up at CUNY or HESC. "You need to be with people whose lives you can enrich," he told me, knowing full well I always was looking for opportunities where I could lead as a teacher.

Telling him about the opportunity made me think about Uncle Sam's enduring question: "Dolores, how does what you're doing help Negroes? What are you doing for the community?" At Chicago State, we could use what we had learned about the power of information to provide a sense of identity to students, a common base, I said. We would be clear about a vision to transform the university and create a home for students.

Of course, my administrative style could take some getting used to for the people at Chicago State. College administrators often look for leaders who are managers with a traditional "let's clean it up, tidy the processes, dot the *I*s and cross the *T*s" style. People had been thrown when they realized I valued teaching and learning among all the members of a team, myself most emphatically included. Dennis and I both knew people were not always comfortable with my style, especially if they were not in tune with my passion and my way as a teacher, intent on engaging people.

"Dennis, I am still a teacher, and I view you as my trainer, helping me stay the course," I said. "You've been there help-ing me hear what others are feeling. You've been there as a col-league who was not afraid to challenge me or help others as we learned together and created a community." In Claremont, he was the student who had fully comprehended the model I was conveying of being a willing student, teacher and leader all the time. He was the one who described me to colleagues as always being 30 seconds ahead of myself in thought. Sometimes I jumped from the spoken words based on a thought that was there 30 seconds ago and pick up at the thought that was there 30 seconds later, producing gaps. This could be an annoying mannerism, causing me to lose people, until they got to know me or call me on it. I expected people to run fast with me. Dennis and I were always on pace.

Our conversation turned to him and what it would be like if he continued at the University of Minnesota. Accustomed to working with me, he realized he could keep things moving by checking in with me long distance to assure our actions were in sync and that we were continuing to learn from each other. He felt he needed to stay to finish the work he had started and, more important, to keep Elke, who was ill, in a now-familiar place.

Dennis promised to come to Chicago for my inauguration and share with the CSU community the circle of learning so that they would know what to expect from me. "Dolores, be yourself," he said, urging me not to wait too long to communi-cate who I was and to share my vision at my inaugural address.

In Chicago, U.S. Education Secretary William Bennett had damned the Chicago Public School system. We heard so little about the potential of our urban youth. Many students who could have benefitted from Chicago State University, many students who should have been given a chance, had been dis-couraged. We had to get beyond the discouragement factor and get the university on course.

I drew on what I had learned from my experience: do not be captive to how an institution is perceived; rather, make it what you want it to be. My mother dared to be different, and now my children were successful on their own, learning from me and teaching me as they went. Tom Jr. was a self-assured, unconventional teacher, with no regrets about the course of his life. Jane had said no to a career in corporate law and was intent on finding a role that matched her spirit. And I drew from my ancestors who as slaves had taught themselves to read and write.

It was at the Fall Convocation in 1990 that I spoke to the CSU community about the road I envisioned us traveling together. Student retention and academic success are our top priorities, I said. We must dramatically increase the graduation and first-year student retention rates. At the time, only 18 percent of our first-time freshmen completed their degrees in five years. I asked the faculty and staff to set a goal of graduating a significantly larger percentage of our students in seven years. I also asked them to establish a goal— drive up the percentage of first-year students returning for a second year.

As I stood before the faculty and staff occupying the seats and standing along the walls in CSU's Robinson University Center, I recalled the pledge I had made to the Board of Governors of State Colleges and Universities when they appointed me as CSU's president on May 18, 1990. I pledged to them to improve student access, retention and graduation rates, all indicators of student success. I wanted our students to experience constructive academic intervention, committed leadership and a supportive environment.

Over a two-month period, at a series of eight retreats, faculty, staff, administrators and students engaged in discussions to establish and clarify the university's goals. I talked with each group for seven to ten minutes on what we wanted to achieve as a university and then invited them to discuss their ideas and concerns in smaller groups. Each of the groups appointed a reporter to tell me their ideas. I wanted to model an interactive approach and keep the focus on the big picture. The groups proposed a variety of retention and student success initiatives that included: advancing minority participation in higher education; strengthening graduate and undergraduate programs; promoting assistance to public schools through pre-college initiatives; collaborating with other institutions of higher learning for mutual benefit; and providing service to the community. We called this the CSU model for student success.

Across the campus, the momentum was building. We were coming together to create and support shared goals. We shared a passion, a force that was propelling us to a level of innovation beyond the conventional. We had started to build a community at CSU.

The bottom line for me was that we would provide access for qualified students, support them so that they could grow and succeed academically and personally, and then make sure they graduated. How we helped to shape and mold those students was important. Would our graduates be able to make a difference in their communities, the state and the nation? Would they strive to understand and appreciate all people? Would they understand that we are all each other's keepers? Our efforts would mean little if we produced students who wanted to be part of a culture of greed and corruption, or if we produced clones of corporate and political mediocrity. Our mission had to be to send back to our communities and nation creative thinkers who understood how to be change agents and community builders.

At my official inauguration ceremony several months after Convocation, I looked around at the hundreds of people seated in the auditorium at Navy Pier. As I made my way down the center aisle with Illinois Governor Jim Edgar by my side, I reflected on the previous months and the momentum we had already built within the CSU community. I, along with Dennis, whom I had invited to speak, would share our circle of learning concept with the community. I felt humble as I made my way to the stage.

"Chicago State University represents a collage of people involved in teaching and learning, involved in a renewal process fueled by our individual and collective will to achieve all we are capable of achieving. A university must be defined

in terms of its faculty, administrators, staff and, most important, its students," I said. We had to understand what was necessary to succeed as individuals, as a family and as a community of people and learn from each other.

As I had at CUNY and HESC, I identified part of my
administrative team from within, drawing from their knowledge of the institution and the Illinois Board of Governors of
State Colleges and Universities system. I also brought in someone from the outside with yet another perspective, Susan
Lourenco. While she was at the University of Illinois, she had
championed many of the same things I had in other environ-
ments. A white Jewish woman, she was proof there is no one
group defined by race, culture, language or gender that has a
monopoly on a passionate commitment to working to ensure
opportunities for people.

As president of CSU and a teacher, I wanted to show that
barriers are artificial when individuals share the same goals. I
felt that Susan, whom I had known professionally for more
than twenty years, could help. I, of course, anticipated the
question that indeed arose about her presence: "Who is this
white Jewish woman, and why is she senior advisor to the
president?" I focused on what my grandmother had said so
often, "Your friends will understand and your enemies won't
believe you anyway."

While my administrative team evolved, I began to cultivate external supporters and individuals who would cheer us
on, respect us for where we had come from and wanted to go,
and who had a stake in our success. As I did with the internal
university community, I had to get outside groups to understand our students, the institution and my vision. I met with
many wonderful individuals from Chicago's various neighborhoods, CSU's alumni body, the Chicago religious community,
and citywide and local organizations. I also also forged relationships on a national level, becoming involved in the
American Council on Education as well as the American
Association of State Colleges and Universities. I reveled in
telling CSU's story to everyone.

During my tenure, supporters emerged among legislators, the immediate and larger community, and corporate and business leaders. One group that became critically important to the success of our students was the President's Council of Community Volunteers.

The Council, primarily made up of retired individuals, provided a wealth of services, including mentoring, tutoring and exam proctoring.

One day, I got a call from a woman by the name of Janet Morrow, who asked me to join the Chicago Metro Ethics Coalition. She spoke of her values and the diverse groups she was part of. I don't recall how she'd found me, but I liked what I heard and agreed to attend a meeting. I felt a bond as she spoke of her involvement with individuals as diverse as those who attended the coalition meetings, but who also addressed issues of personal and spiritual growth. She came to CSU to hear our story and share what she had learned on how groups protect and develop values. Janet's husband was Richard Morrow, CEO and chairman of Amoco.

At a lunch meeting she arranged for women friends who were CEOs or spouses of CEOs, she introduced me to Jane Perkins. Jane's experiences with being divorced earlier in her life and going it alone were similar to my own. She understood my passion for CSU and suggested I meet with her husband, Don Perkins. Former CEO and chairman of Jewel Foods, Don was on several corporate boards. We met for breakfast, and I shared the CSU story, why the university was important to Chicago, the potential and determination the students possessed, and why the university mattered so much to so many. Don heard with both his heart and mind. He could relate to the challenge from his own experience of finding his way to Yale University and not having much support at home. The corporate community, he agreed, would have to be convinced that CSU students were a good investment.

Within a few minutes, he suggested engaging the business community by creating a new group, Friends of CSU Scholars. Talented students would be matched with corporate mentors whom he personally would recruit. He knew that showing students doing their personal best would win corporate support. This became one of many efforts where collaborative partnerships between the university and the external community were instrumental in helping students succeed.

Many of the people I met as president did more than help the university. They also helped me, providing me with reserves of goodwill and support that I could draw upon when I felt my energy running low. One such person was Chicago entrepreneur Jacoby Dickens. Jacoby, chairman of the board of Seaway Bank on Chicago's South Side, had made a fortune in real estate, bowling alleys and banking after working for 14 years as an engineer for the Chicago Board of Education. Like Don Perkins, Jacoby brought to the table a network of contacts he called upon to assist students. He also contributed his personal time, mentoring and speaking to students about experiences that shaped his life. Again and again, Jacoby showed his commitment to CSU, counseling me and sometimes admonishing me to develop a tougher skin. Before I left the university, Jacoby pledged a million-dollar gift to the institution, the largest gift an individual has ever made to CSU. In announcing his gift, Jacoby spoke of the importance of education and expressed his hope that his gift would inspire others to give.

I usually got to campus by 5:30 or 6 o'clock each morning to train alone or run with the track team. Running gave me the metaphor to express the commitment we needed to transform the university. In my first semester as president, I initiated the first CSU 5K walk-run, which brought faculty, students and the community to the track and inspired runners around the campus. More than 700 people participated in that event, which we called "Educate Your Body, Educate Your Mind."

Leading by example, I completed that first of eight annual 5K runs during the course of my presidency in just 23 minutes, achieving first place in the 50-to-55 age category. And I trained as well for my first Chicago Marathon—my sixth overall. I placed in the top ten in my age category.

Achieving all of our goals at CSU was not an easy task. We moved forward on many fronts, while sliding backwards on others. In addition to not having enough state funds to begin with, we faced a potential federal financial aid audit disallowance of nearly $4 million. Through hard work, we managed to get that amount reduced to $300,000. We also had to reallocate dollars from administration to meet additional instructional costs due to increased enrollments. Overall, we had to do more with less.

Surviving as an institution meant we had to be resilient and resourceful. Changing technology needs, new federal and state reporting requirements, new accounting procedures, the need for compliance with audit findings at various levels and challenges in maintaining our infrastructure all were putting pressure on the bottom line. Furthermore, our faculty compensation was inequitable. CSU faculty were among the lowest paid in the state, yet they had the highest teaching load. After negotiations increased faculty salaries, we put a freeze on vacant positions and equipment purchases and reduced overtime and extra help budgets. Sacrifice was the order of the day. Two steps forward, one step back. We had to keep reminding ourselves that even with the dismal budget scenario we were moving forward with our commitment to students.

Five years into my presidency, I began to see signs that our strides were slowing and our energy waning. I knew there were individuals within the CSU community who felt our efforts were futile. An English professor accused me of being out of touch. It was a sad wake-up call: not everyone in the CSU family believed that access, equity and quality are compatible.

Gwendolyn Brooks, poet laureate of Illinois, wrote a poem in my honor in December 1991. Titled "Captain Dolores," the poet spoke about my determination, tenacity and administrative style:

CAPTAIN DOLORES

Like Nature

Captain Dolores italicizes Positives.

In this world
she will not allow assault, betrayal, trivia
to alter her View of herself, of her mission.

She reaches beyond calamity.

Captain Dolores mesmerizes her milieu.
She confronts and pushes back
all Nothing, all hazardous Nothing rolling
silently toward!

Where there was negligible sound,
now there is music sponsored and valid;
various, agreeable, ranging.

Captain Dolores—
explicit, apprehendable, clean!
Map-maker. Resource Center.

Symbol of the Engaged Hand.

Being bold, as I think Ms. Brooks defined me, in some
ways cost the university as a whole and exhausted and dis-
couraged some people. Our continued serious fiscal challenges
combined with administrative changes that were misunder-
stood and even downright unconventional sapped people's
resiliency. The governance of the university also changed,
going from my reporting to a board that governed five universities to a local board focusing exclusively on CSU.

At some point in every challenged organization, it

becomes time for the leader to consider moving out of the way and clearing the way for new leadership. I did not want Dolores Cross to become the issue or the agenda. In spite of what some wanted to think, the issue remained that of equity and access. The agenda continued to be one of finding ways to meet the needs of the university's unique student population and the needs of the community the university served. The lessons I had learned in my life were no different from those faced by the university and by me as its head. We had been able to withstand our difficulties, given our mission and changing demographics, by learning the art of changing with the times.

In 1992, I defined what I would view as my CSU legacy: the establishment of the Gwendolyn Brooks Center for Black Literature and Creative Writing. In addition to creating and allocating permanent space for the Gwendolyn Brooks Center, the student union and the residence hall were constructed and opened a few years later. They bore a distinctive architectural style that reflected the African roots of the majority of CSU students. We also built an addition to the university's science center, completed a multi-million-dollar technology infrastructure project to link all the buildings on the campus and open up student computer laboratories around the campus, established a Women's Resource Center, a Wellness Center and a state-of-the-art Fitness Center for students, faculty, staff and community.

Our community relationships were strong. The CSU Community Volunteers Council, which worked directly with me, included 107 volunteers. The CSU Clergy Council, 50 clergy strong, helped us to inform the community of student concerns. The Women's Advisory Council, consisting of women leaders from CSU as well as corporate, civic and government sectors, advised and mentored students. And of course, we had Don Perkins' brainchild, the Friends of CSU Scholars.

We received local, state and national recognition for success in student advocacy efforts, innovative retention strategies, institutional development, public relations, community service and networking. We held the community together in spite of our internal struggles. We helped students achieve.

MILE 25.7

Runners understand this: Once the race begins, you may never turn around and retrace your steps. You may never return to the starting line. You have to keep pushing forward, even if your time is slow or the course unimaginably difficult. You may stop there, to run another day, but it is impossible to go back to where you started.

My extended family at CSU included my driver and my housekeeper. For some time, they were the only ones who knew of my friendship with a Chicagoan, James Willis. We shared interests in nutrition, health, sports and his vocation as a jazz musician. I met James when he volunteered to be part of a community group mentoring, assisting and supporting the university in a range of service projects.

Our relationship developed as he began stopping by the residence with information on supplements and training as I prepared for races and upcoming marathons. He also offered to come by to make a salad. I watched him, not sure what to make of it all and not tuned in to his way of courting. A salad and a conversation on training, supplements, activities and concerns and CSU worries—in all, a good night. I called him when I was in Atlanta on business to tell him that I would be running the Boston Marathon in April, which was earlier in the year than I usually run a marathon. Would he be a sort of trainer to me? I asked. His enthusiasm came through the phone lines very clearly. Later I learned that he had almost done flips. He had posted a picture of me in his apartment, hoping for a breakthrough. Initially, I wasn't sure what I wanted to come of the relationship, but the friendship felt comfortable and I was clear that I did not want folks to be distracted with gossip about Dr. Cross and a MAN. I was deep into my independence in showing that I didn't need anyone in my life.

I liked the way he made me laugh and how we'd find humor in most things. I liked the feeling of having fun and being with someone who accepted and thought well of me. He didn't try to make me over. He found me attractive, interesting and was not threatened by me. We went for a run around Washington Park. I circled the park two times to his single circle, and he admired and bragged about what I had done. I was able to raise the fitness bar with him as we tackled steep hills when cycling or venture off to new territory. He took a compass on our trips after he learned that I liked to dart out not knowing where I was going, only to get lost. I did not admit my feelings for him. In my mind, we were too different. How could he possibly understand my world and the depth of my involvement?

Our trip to Boston for the marathon was not easy. I was not comfortable with our spending the night together and kept changing rooms, looking for enough space. Yet I let him give me a massage and felt such caring and tenderness in his touching. It was very confusing. I was reluctant to let other runners from Chicago know he was my companion at the event.

As I took off, a good feeling swept over me as I realized he would be there at the finish line. He had come to see me through in the challenge of Boston.

By mile twelve, I realized I had started off too fast. I could barely answer when a young woman runner approached me after reading my CSU shirt. She introduced herself as Gail Vanderheide, confiding that she had seen an article on me in *Runner's World* and admired what I was achieving at CSU. Her conversation got me through. We finished in 3 hours and 57 minutes with a promise that I would join her and colleagues in the Hood-to-Coast Relay in Oregon later that year.

After that marathon, I knew James would be more than a friend. James instinctively knew my mother would not be easy about this relationship, so he brought his bass over when he met her. He played for her, made up songs, and won her reluctant approval.

He viewed himself as supplying the Band-Aids I needed after dealing with student protests, union issues, administrative misunderstandings and bombs launched by the faculty. At times, he said he was worried about running out of Band-Aids, when I seemed to return home with more scrapes and cuts. At night sometimes I couldn't sleep or wouldn't eat or I simply showed no interest in anything but CSU. He heard the concern in my tone as I spoke on the phone to Jane, getting a second opinion on a campus matter from her. I was aware of his devotion and his putting some of his own aspirations on hold.

James would hear and share what he knew of community awareness of my leadership at Chicago State University. He picked up bits of chatter at the CSU Fitness Center, the barber shop or a meeting of community volunteers. As people began to realize our relationship, they used James to get a message to me. Sensitive to my load, he was selective in what he would share. In his view, there were people close to me who were not watching my back, not as loyal as perhaps I had hoped. We argued as I asserted I would not give up, to which he commented with concern, "Just look at how it's kicking your butt."

Every day, I worked to promote CSU in the community. A September 1993 column by Clarence Page in the *Chicago Tribune* hit home for me. "Perhaps most of all we need to study the ghetto successes, not just its failures. We have something to learn from low-income teens who are not in gangs, on drugs or pregnant out of wedlock. They are a majority of the poor, but they are invisible. When we agonize over our failures and ignore our successes, the result is more despair, a growing sense that no solutions work. We've learned plenty about what doesn't work. Let's study what does."

Many of CSU's students came from circumstances not unlike those of the people making the headlines in stories of youth violence. The difference was that someone cared about them and there was a university in the community intent on their succeeding. I wrote a commentary that CSU was a study of what works. And I wrote another about what the university was doing for young people through the Triathlon program. Run by Bernard Lyles, an extraordinary young black male, the program involved close to 100 young people ages 9 through 16 in sports in a university environment.

The inequities we still see today have always been there, I said. Their reality cannot constrain or paralyze us. We must move ahead and salute success. We must encourage people with positive interventions and recognize that you don't have to have a title to lead or follow. All you have to have is the will. We must not behave as if action arises from nothingness or as if there is not a base from which to proceed. Saying that it is too late, too difficult, or, even more, saying that there is nothing upon which to build sends a destructive message.

Where will you go if you deny the tracks in the sand made by your predecessors? I was proud to be making tracks myself. And getting on with my life.

Tom Jr.'s call announcing his engagement and proposed wedding date came out of the blue. While I knew he had been dating and having great fun with Patricia Kelly, I had no idea how serious they had become. They met shortly after he had moved to Minneapolis from California to teach music in the Mineapolis Public Schools. He was living with Jane in my house on Bryant Street while Jane worked on her doctorate at the University of Minnesota and as a graduate assistant in academic support.

In Patricia, Tommy found a strong woman proud of her Irish heritage and her home state of Minnesota. She viewed her relationship with Tom as a challenge, yet her surprise was clear as heads turned when she and Tom held hand or embraced in public. I questioned whether or not Pat was enlightened about the tough road for black men in this country, and I found myself breaking the ice by giving her books on the black experience, such as Cornell West's *Race Matters*.

When Tommy called to tell me that they were getting married, I somehow felt I missed out on the discussion I always thought we would have. I had envisioned a mother-son conversation in which I would listen, acknowledge her fine qualities and then hold his hands in mine and ask: "Tommy, do you really want to marry a white woman? Do you really want to take on the problems of an interracial marriage? Son, don't you have enough problems as a young black man in this country without being locked, arm-in-arm, with a white woman?" If given the opportunity, I would have gone on about how "white folks are not ready. They will smile and be 'Minnesota nice,' but when it comes to getting tenure as a teacher, your interracial marriage will be an unspoken aspect of the evaluation." But it was past time for that heart-to-heart conversation. And he knew that, despite my concerns, I would support his choice. The wedding was on, and I jokingly threatened not to come to the big day but to be there for the "divorce celebration."

As the mother of the groom, my challenge was to see that family and friends would be there—and to find a drop-dead gorgeous dress. I would be coming to terms with seeing Tom Sr. and his wife, Lynn, as a couple. Alice Murphy had described Lynn and me as flavors of ice cream. "Dee, as a black woman, you are chocolate and Lynn, as a white woman, is vanilla." This was Alice's way of saying that Tom's wife and I shared some qualities and, under different circumstances, might even be buddies.

The wedding brought us all together. The Murphys, Alice, Paul, and their children, Karann, Pat and his wife, and Allie and his wife. The McRaes, my sister, Jean, and her husband, Jake, and their children Karen, Steven and Tina. Tom's cousin Steven. And, of course, my mother and my friends James Willis, Eunice Holder, Mary Hazel, Susan and Louise Lourenco and her husband Louie Williams, and Dennis and Elke Cabral. I felt they were there as much to support me as to be a part of the wedding festivities.

From our first encounter that weekend, Tom and I closed ranks as the parents of the groom and related to each other as if the divorce had not happened. There were tender moments as we walked alone, recalling his displeasure when Tommy elected to play in the band instead of play basketball and how Tommy had, at age seven, knocked down Tom's trophy case. We remembered with a laugh how both of us had been unsure whether Tommy wanted to be a lifelong undergraduate at Sonoma. We both cried during the church wedding and stood together in the receiving line. Our time together was extended on the dance floor, and we spoke of those moments as a "final releasing with love, a moving on" for both of us. My mother attempted a distraction from our deep conversation by dancing with her grandson, the groom. Jean engaged Lynn in a discussion as if she were a long lost friend. Jane finally came up to dance with her father. Alice commented, "This is just like old times."

Tommy and Patricia were ecstatic, enjoying the families coming together, behaving themselves. The families were mixing, dancing and having a grand time.

MILE 25.8

The last long, real run before a marathon is three weeks ahead of the crack of the starter's pistol. This is when you must listen closer than ever to the body that carries you 60 miles a week. This is when you pull everything you have—body and soul—together to meet the challenge.

It was 5:30 a.m., Monday, April 15, and for the fourteenth time, I was preparing to run the 26.2 mile distance of a marathon. This marathon was to be like no other. It was the 100th running of the Boston Marathon, with a field of more than 38,500 runners, making it the world's largest marathon. Boston has always been a no-nonsense marathon. A woman in my 55-to-59 age category must be able to complete the 26.2 miles in under four hours, five minutes to qualify. In 1992, I completed Boston in less than four hours. My best marathon time was three hours, 37 minutes. For this year, in Boston, I had acquired lottery number, 31403, from a good friend. According to organizers, 32,000 runners had to be turned away.

I was committed to going the distance and determined to do it right. Of immediate concern, however, was getting to the starting area with everything I needed: hat, gloves, Vaseline, aspirin, pins, a shirt I could throw away when I needed to, tissues, an electronic running chip in my shoe for tracking and the bib with my racing number, 31403, pinned to my shirt. In a normal marathon, I would be running alone in my usual symbolic "I am woman" solitary survivor mode. For this historic occasion, I was running with the Oregon runner I met at the 96th running of Boston Marathon, Gail Vanderheide, and her friend Linda Gallon, also from Oregon. We planned to run for the fun and joy of the historic moment, to be together, to help each other get through the grueling hills from Hopkington to Boston.

The logistical challenge began with our having to beat the congestion to meet at the buses, since we all were at different hotels. Full of the quiet excitement of an early race-day morning, the crowd was orderly, in good humor and in awe of the arrangements made to accommodate the massive movement of runners on what seemed to be a perfect running day, cool now and only expected to be 55 degrees by noon. We boarded the bus at 7 a.m. to head into the small rural town of Hopkington. We were told 800 buses were ferrying people from Boston. The number running was four times the population of Hopkington. The conversation on the bus centered on marathons we'd completed, our injuries, best racing times, length of our long runs, speed and hill work, stretching, hydrating and adapting to the stress of a marathon. There was little risk of boring fellow travelers with the travails of our running addiction.

The 40-minute ride to the start area was extended to two hours when one of the buses broke down. The wait meant that some of us had to disembark and run for the woods for a minute to relieve ourselves. We finally pulled up to Athletes Village shortly after 9 a.m. and patiently followed a stretch of runners through mud and matted grass to the tents where we looked for a place to wait out the two-and-a-half hours until noon. We settled on an area in front of the band shell where we heard speakers refer to this year's Boston Marathon as the Woodstock of distance running. The title seemed apropos as the music started and runners clapped, danced and sang, "I Will Survive." Then we went on to the pre-race finishing touches of covering the legs, arms and feet with Vaseline, drinking plenty of water and discussing how we would get to the start line relaxed, focused and ready for what we regarded as a 26.2-mile running party.

The huge contingent of runners from all over the world listened to and followed the directions blared through the sound system. It was uncannily calm. Forty thousand people moving like 40, calm, almost spiritual. For me the thought was of the pilgrimage that had gotten me to the start of this marathon. The long hours of training, cross-training, focusing and trying not to let other stresses impede my progress.

At 11:45 a.m. the wheelchair division started. At 12 noon, we heard the gun go off. We proceeded slowly down the narrow two-lane highway in Hopkington. It would be a half-hour before we would reach the start and an additional 20 minutes before we could run at a slow pace. We would be moving against the wind for the next 26.2 miles. The mood of the spectators and the runners was wonderful—encouraging, supportive and celebratory. The sun was warm, spirits were high and the road ahead was thick with bobbing heads. It was an awesome sight.

Marathon Day in Boston was also Patriot's Day, a state holiday that commemorating the ride of Paul Revere. There was a picnic atmosphere filling our senses—music in our ears, barbecue smells, colorfully dressed spectators and vistas to enjoy. The people lining the street reached out to slap our hands as we went by.

Gail, Linda and I took turns assuming a lead pace, which often meant weaving our way through groups of people. We chattered and read T-shirts as we ran:

> "In Memory of Mom"
> "It's All Attitude"
> "Like Father"
> "Race for the Cure"
> "Race for Research"
> "I"m 50 and Eligible"
> "My Feet Hurt"

My singlet read "Chicago State University," and it was encouraging to hear people shout "Go Chicago State!" We stopped often for water, and less often, for pit stops. We regarded the marathon as a test of endurance and were determined to get to the finish line feeling good. We ran miles 2 through 10 at a very slow 10-minute-mile pace, took a 10-minute bathroom stop and began running 8-9-10-minute-mile intervals. We were running smoothly, feeling well-paced and positive. We gave each mile the respect it deserved.

The checkpoint on how well we'd feel at the finish became apparent at about mile 15, near Wellesley College. We knew from running Boston in 1992 that the enthusiasm of the Wellesley women would help us face the grueling Heartbreak Hill. I felt Heartbreak Hill would be a challenge, but not as devastating as it was in 1992. My extensive cross-training, weight work and hill repeats would pay off, I felt. We ran the uninterrupted course heading toward the hill at a pace anywhere from 8 to 10 minutes a mile, having fun taking turns in the lead and watching out for each other.

Running with Gail and Linda helped me persevere. Strong marathoners, each had completed more than 25 marathons, with best times under three-and-a-half hours and qualifying for Boston in the 45 to 49 age category. Their decision to run a slower marathon bonded us together and made me feel grateful. The conversation among the three of us ran the gamut from the beautiful countryside to where we wanted our ashes sprinkled when we died. We continually came back to the wonderful crowd that cheered us on, fed us orange slices and cookies, and offered Vaseline and sponges.

People sang to us, played for us. They were old, young, men, women and of various cultures—running and watching. I saw T-shirts from Japan, Mexico, Sweden, Ireland, England, Kenya, China and Korea and from states throughout the United States. I was pleased to encounter two runners from Chicago who knew of Chicago State. After two hours, 10 minutes into the race, we were told who won the Marathon. It felt great to share a race with the world's best. There are few sports in which you can compete with the elite.

We approached Heartbreak Hill at a slow pace, chugging along without a stop. Despite all my training, I felt a slight aggravation in my shin. I focused on moving ahead as I stopped for a second and put three aspirin in my mouth. Not even for a brief moment did I worry about making it. I heard, "You can do it," "Keep it up," "Looking good," and "Go, soul sister."

The long race gave me time to think about and deeply appreciate the generosity of my friend Meg Reeves for my place in the marathon; Evelyn Murphy, the former Lieutenant Governor of Massachusetts, marathoner and my long-time friend, who gave me her sweatshirt to get me through the cold morning wait in Hopkington; and my other friends and family. While they weren't there lining the streets of Boston, they gave me support that saw me through. "I'm proud of you, Mom" and "Ma, I know you'll do great," from my children. "Good luck baby, love ya," from my mother. "Dee, I knew you'd be in it," from Jean.

"Dr. Cross, you're strong and ready" and "Dolores, don't forget the post-race party!" from others.

I experienced the wonder of being there and the power of a positive energy that took me beyond worrying about making it to the joy and pleasure of doing it. The action of running feet striking heel-toe, arms swinging low, hands open, breathing quietly, made me experience a clarity, a clearer self.

By mile 20, however, we began to feel the stress of running against the wind as the temperature began to drop. My body got cold. My fingers were numb. I worried about hypothermia. The conversation moved to, "How're you doing?" "You okay?" "Let's stay together, we're doing it." At times, I just wanted quiet—no talk—just focus. Gail helped me by encouraging me to use my arms. By mile 25, I began to seek out benchmarks. Make it to the traffic light. Make it to the bridge. Make it to the tree. Feet, don't fail me now. Again, I was greatly helped by people calling out, "You're almost there." I felt my form was good, well-paced.

Despite the cold, I pushed ahead on automatic, appreciative of the crowd. That crowd had been standing out there for nearly five hours, no mean feat.

The finish line appeared as a glorious sight, an orange and blue banner stretched across four lanes of street in downtown Boston. We had made it—from rural Hopkington to busy Boston in under five hours.

Gail, Linda and I joined hands and raised our arms—big

smiles—for our photo-perfect finish. An historic moment for us—winners, finishers and friends. The announcer read the name on my shirt; "Dolores Cross," he shouted, expressing my jubilance aloud. We proceeded down the long chute slowly, helped by one of the many volunteers who had been there for us throughout the long day. We were given blankets and directed to the buses where we picked up our warm-ups and personal supplies. And then we went to receive our blue-and-gold finishers' medals. We were in about middle of the pack, having come in under five hours. The last finisher came in three hours later.

We had proved to our minds and bodies that we could meet the challenges of the colossal 100th running of Boston. A dream come true. I ask myself, was it worth it? Would I, number 31403, do it again?

Yes! Yes! Yes! Yes!

I ran two additional marathons in 1996, Portland in October with Gail, and just three weeks later, Chicago. I completed the Chicago marathon at age 59 in less time than I had run my first marathon at age 50.

MILE 26

After the running is done, it is difficult to tread lightly again.

"Dolores, you cannot do everything," my mother scolded. "When are you going to take a rest?" I could not imagine a time when I wouldn't have my mother to respond to what I was doing and interject her concerns. It just didn't fully register with me that my mother's health was declining, until my sister called to tell me that Ma had to be taken to the hospital. Even then, I felt she would be tended to and be home again in the care of my sister shortly. Jean asked me to come to New Jersey that weekend so she and Jake could go to their youngest daughter's graduation from Hampton College.

"Hi, gorgeous," Ma said as I entered her hospital room. "Gorgeous yourself," I said. I had visited her in the hospital before, but not under these circumstances. I suddenly felt I had gotten there too late. Too late, in that I felt I had no magic, no words, no suggestions to help her. In her mind, she still was experiencing the endlessness of primetime. My mother did not in her 60s think it inappropriate, or too late, to go to school. I heard her envision her next job when she was in her 70s. She avoided what she considered to be "middle age" outfits.

She'd been diagnosed with a urinary tract infection. There were tubes everywhere, making it difficult for her to move. She asked about Jane and Tom Jr. in the usual ways that didn't acknowledge that they were adults and very much on their own. She inquired about their health and wanted details on how they were taking care of themselves. They were her babies, just as I was still her little girl. Her conversations with me suggested that she believed somehow I'd fooled them all, all of the people in my professional adult life, with my bright eyes and big smile. I had quietly slipped past my sister's energetic personality and fooled everyone.

I asked her if she wanted me to read or sing. "Sing," she

grinned. I began with a song she sang often when I was a child. "My dessert is waiting," I warbled, mimicking the way she let her voice quiver. She laughed and joined in with the words I had forgotten. When I started singing, "Don't you feel my legs or you might get high …" her response was just as I heard it almost 50 years before. "Henry should not have taught you those songs!" she said.

When I visited her the next day, she cried about how the nurses had hurt her after she had an incision in her neck to allow them to clear fluid from her lungs. She was angry and in pain. The pain quickly grew worse, and the nurses said she probably had an infection. A young nurse asked me, "How old is your mother?" But I heard in her tone the unspoken "perhaps she's old enough to die." I didn't respond, but she saw in my face and in my silence my anger. I demanded they find her doctor, and they hurried out, leaving me with Ma.

She was breathing hard, heaving, with her eyes closed. Every breath was a struggle and required her to focus. My mother had no plans to go gently into the night. She was fighting—rather, fighting again. In her face, I saw resignation, yet determination to continue her battle. That same expression shaped her face when she fought for her denied civil service title and when she reacted to the mutilation of Emmet Till as if he had been her son. She had a life of fighting. Each breath was her will to live another day to make a difference.

How seldom had I heard my mother speak of retiring and finding that place in the sun! She kept herself reacting at a fever pitch, making sure she heard the news and talking back to the television, reading the newspaper and judging the reporting, carefully reading and re-reading every press clip I had sent her and imagining the impact.

While I watched her breathe, I thought of her recent admonitions to me. When I was a child, she wanted to influence me to go on to ever higher and higher levels. But now she was trying to influence me, if that were possible, to "find some time for yourself," to "rest" and to have more time for her as well. I suddenly regretted that I'd let the business of the university keep me from those visits she'd wanted. I absorbed myself in the moments at hand.

In reality, I could not have answered the nurse's "What is your mother's age?" I didn't know. My mother, in some game, had not let us know precisely. The year would change to suit her. "If folks know your age, they'll tell you when to die," she said. "It's nobody's business." Sometime in her 70s, when she still drove a car, she had a job delivering food to senior citizens. She took much delight in their treatment of her as a "young thing." She also refused to live in a senior citizens housing project, because she felt it would depress her being around old people. She was most comfortable engaging her grandchildren in a debate or taking on her son-in-law, Jake. She was known for taking the opposite position just to be engaged. But she drew the line on taking the position of staunch conservatives.

The doctor came and explained the procedure they'd undertaken. Her airway had been obstructed by a growth. He confided that her prospects did not look good. I turned to see my mother fighting to get her breath and wanted her to win yet another fight.

I returned to Chicago to get clothes and prepare to stay longer. When I reached Chicago, my sister called advising me to take the next plane back. I returned to find my mother had already died.

The days before the funeral were a blur. I went through her papers, her clippings of every step I had made. There were programs from graduations, ticket stubs from football games in Ann Arbor, clippings from Tom Sr.'s basketball days, and of course, there were photos that she had somehow managed to get from my possession. I found cards she'd intended to send me. One of the cards contained a crumpled dollar bill. I saw her life in the piles of papers on her court case and lawsuit.

One letter implored her lawyer to reopen her case. There was evidence of the various stages of her fight, her disappointment and anguish. And her papers revealed her days as a young mother going to night school, taking civil service exams and writing as a reporter for the *Afro American News*. Her articles reflected the achievements of Negroes. She had no time to talk of failures or to imagine us as anything but a strong people and a wronged people. I saw no love letters yet I knew there had been men in her life. I don't remember her lamenting the absence of a man.   I saw how much my life and my achievements had meant to her.

At her funeral, we each spoke of my mother.   Tom Jr. talked her being a "terror" behind the wheel of a car as she ranted on about the news of the day and swerved in traffic. Jane read a poem.   Karen reminded us all that we stand on her shoulders, an observation that annoyed me for some reason.   I read what Ma had written about her life in Raleigh, her growing up, her marriage and her pride in her daughters and their children.

I felt at her passing my own moving on, a coming of age and a fearing of age. I felt 60 and remembered that my father had died at 61.

Losing my mother made everything feel meaningless. She was my audience, my coach. I was part of her team, the star. I started out fighting for her, to give her a feeling of accomplishment in the face of her disappointments. And then at some point I'd gone on to another level, enjoying the pitch and pace of my life, remaining connected to the past while experiencing a present that was new ground for her and my family.

I returned to Chicago and was overwhelmed by the cards and outpouring from the community. They knew me as a daughter and identified with my grief. They had connected with her. As I opened their cards and read their wishes, I heard my mother say, as she did when she felt others were taking credit for me, "I am your mother. I want to be respected as your mother." I felt my mother smiling as the cards, calls and letters related her to me and acknowledged that ours was a special relationship. The guilt was difficult to bear when I thought about how I let myself get involved in university crises and postponed trips to see her. I tried to stay ahead of my bereavement by delving into my work. I was avoiding the message of her death.

My mother's story is a story of success. Even more, it is a reflection of how you can overcome the odds and use adversities as blocks from which to build.

MILE 26.01

When you're in a marathon, you find years in minutes, whole lives in city blocks. You try to appreciate the sweet moments when time follows your lead. Get the rhythm. Relax. Release. Relate. Whether you're running, walking or in a wheelchair, you realize that breaking through the wall is part of your present and your past. You know you can do it again.

I regarded the call from a corporate-based foundation on the East Coast as a message from my mother: "Move on. Move on. The job at Chicago State has required too much of you." But even more, I viewed the offer to become president of this foundation as an unmatched opportunity to reassess, reflect and keep moving. It was time for a change, time to come to terms with the fact that everything must end sometime.

In my leadership at CSU, some people felt pushed and not appreciated, while others were worn down from having to keep others pumped up and still tend to their jobs. They needed me to go and permit a revitalization, a revitalization that happens when there is change at the top.

Chicago State University had been my life for more than seven years. I was leaving a different campus than I found when I arrived. Even the landscape had changed. The new student center, with its ethnocentric design, illustrated what CSU was and who it served. I could not look at the building without being reminded of the many sessions around my conference table when we planned this African expression as part of the design. I firmly demanded that the top be shaped like a pyramid with lights so that people from all around could see the new lights and feel the new energy of Chicago State University. Students saw the Adinkra symbols on the floor of the vast atrium and knew they had been created for them.

As I took my last training run around campus, I saw the new residence halls as real homes for our students. I had worried only two years ago that that they might not become a reality. But now I knew our collective legacy had been made real in the "we" tradition.

The "we" tradition that I'd embraced, mindful always of my childhood coaching on the importance of giving back to the community and making a difference for blacks, was captured in a display of photos presented to me by Marcia Best, Sue Gould and the publication team at CSU at a gathering to honor my service at CSU. All those visual memories were there to carry in my heart and share with my children. When I left the celebration, I went home to absorb the history presented in the photos that began with my inauguration and continued to the summer of 1997. There were photos throughout of my mother beaming, images of Jane and Tom Jr. at every major campus event, often with James Willis in the background on his bass.

The university's achievements were captured in faces from the university community. Here was Genevieve Lopardo, who transformed the College of Education and how it related to our urban environment. It was with Genevieve's support that Bartley McSwine initiated the Future Teachers' Club for the university and the greater Chicago area. There was Marva Jolly standing before a wall she'd created on campus, "Old People Say," to capture the wisdom of our ancestors. Ida Bohannon, a retired social worker who visited me early in my tenure, had taken my hand and made a commitment to be there. And there she was, leading the community volunteers and helping to establish the Women's Resource Center. And there were photos of the Black Writer's Conference, an event that was presented to me as a challenge to make happen by the poet and writer Haki Madhubuti. I could never forget the day he introduced me to Gwendolyn Brooks and the pride we all felt as we cut the ribbon for the Gwendolyn Brooks Center at Chicago State. And there were photos as well of Phyllis Overstreet, who added songs from her soul to get us going, and Arlene Olinsky, who would monitor my message of access and opportunity as one campus address led to the next. Rozalyn Brown was there, making sure I "walked the talk" by serving as a mentor to a student. And I saw Marlene Anderson and Yolanda Solarte who, if I seemed stressed, advised me to change into my running clothes and take to the track. Behind every gala and video production was Notre Chatman, whose calm showed even in photographs. The album captured as well my standing tall next to Nelson Mandela during a trip I'd taken with the Council of Foreign Relations to South Africa and my being in the company of Vice Chancellor Ndeble during one of my four trips to the University of the North in South Africa. There I was with President Clinton, Senator Paul Simon, Senator Carol Mosely Braun, U.S. Education Secretary Richard Riley, journalist Vernon Jarrett, State Senator Emil Jones and PUSH leader Jesse Jackson as I reached out to tell the Chicago State University story.

Each page of the album spoke to my running, advancing, moving on, but even more, it captured the Chicago State University story. Somehow I had passed on to others the seriousness of my uncles' question: "How does what we're doing relate to the community and the betterment of Negroes?" I savored the captions. "This president vowed to hit the ground running . . . and she ran . . . and she ran. Dolores Cross is the only president to have more than a 'first annual' anything. And she ran and she ran." The 40-page album concluded "And when she was finished, she started running again."

My time at CSU had been a marathon, a wonderful event, viewed through the lens of a marathoner. Yet I was tired. I didn't want people to see my vulnerabilities. I did not want anyone to know how deep my grief was in leaving CSU. I felt good about the students I helped, the money I raised. We even received $8,000 in contributions for a scholarship in my mother's name. But I did not feel at peace.

A caption under my photo in the *Chicago Sun-Times* read:

A Tough Act to Follow

When Dolores Cross, the only black president of an Illinois public university, heads off to [the East Coast] to begin a new career, she will leave a legacy she can be proud of. At a time when many state-funded universities saw a decline in both retention and graduation rates for African Americans, Chicago State University posted a 57 percent graduation rate. During her seven-year tenure, she steered the university on a strong academic course that brought her and the school national recognition. She will now head up a foundation that distributes $30 million in education grants. Cross, a marathon runner, has set the pace for whomever follows in her footsteps.

My president colleagues in higher education saw the accolades as the right time to leave. "Leave while they love you. It all goes south very fast, and you know for some it has already gone south," Spelman College President Johnnetta Cole told me. I thought of a senior CSU administrator who had gone out of his way to say to a faculty member: "I know that woman, Dolores Cross, was your friend, but she was no administrator."

That remark recalled my conversation with Dennis Cabral some eight years earlier, when he told me that I wouldn't come across as an administrator, especially where people were looking at me strictly as a bureaucrat rather than as manager bringing teaching and learning to my role. "Yes, I'm not your traditional administrator," I said to myself. "I am a teacher and a learner in a management situation, working and doing my personal best, leading people to achieve all they are capable of achieving."

I timed my leaving as president of Chicago State University to include being there for the Chicago State University annual Gala and the eighth running of the Chicago State University 5K. I would be running in the 60-to-64 age category for the first time. It was my last CSU race as its president. I wanted to leave as I had started at CSU, first in my category. And I did—in a time of 23.6 minutes.

The race was September 27, 1997, and I began as president of the foundation October 1, 1997.

What a transition. The physical move from one place to another was complicated because there were relationships to consider. Leaving the Chicago State community, I faced the challenge of managing a long-distance relationship with James. We saw it initially as manageable; love conquers all, we thought. I also wanted a place to live that would accommodate visits from my children. So much of what I had done in my life had not left room for them. My one-bedroom apartment in Manhattan was not going to work after the spaciousness of the president's residence.

I found a condo near the foundation but decided to maintain a two-bedroom apartment in Chicago. While I waited to move into my new condo in late December, I lived out of suitcases, bouncing between my apartment in Manhattan and the foundation guest house.

On my weekends in New York, I worked to put my apartment back together. Aunt Jean's precious sofa had been damaged by my recent tenant. There was a split in the frame and someone had urinated on the cushions. I thought of what my aunt had invested in this furniture. In my busyness, I had not taken care of it.

I found a Jamaican upholsterer. When I took the sofa to him he looked at it with sadness, scooped it up as if it was wounded child and took it away to repair it.

Going to the corporate foundation, I encountered a culture I had not known before. I had been used to seeing so many people of color and now I saw only a few. This new culture forced me to release my love of CSU further and concentrate.

In my first month at the foundation, four of the 10 people there either left for other jobs or retired. By far my biggest challenge was how to create a community within this new culture.

I continued my daily runs to keep my energy high and the blahs at bay. In November, I received an e-mail invitation to participate in the Houston Marathon on January 18, 1998. It became very important for me to run this marathon and register my presence and energy as I sorted things out in the new job.

I had never run a marathon that early in the year. My last marathon had been the New York City Marathon in November

1997. While thunderstorms had made us absolutely miserable, Gail and I prevailed and finished in 4 hours, 35 minutes, better time than in my first New York City Marathon. To prepare for Houston, I maintained a schedule of long runs and took to the hills near my condo to prepare myself for Houston. Training meant I could not enjoy the fun of putting on a few extra holiday pounds or the late-night holiday parties. What's more, training for a marathon is always hard on family and lovers. And for me, the road running came first. There was much at stake. I sent notes to friends announcing that I would do it.

When I met the team in Houston, I learned that, at 60, I was the oldest woman member. I was struck by their youth and their expectations of me. The record for a woman in my 60-to-65 age category had been set in 1987 at 4 hours, 45 minutes. I had no idea where I might finish, given my lack of knowledge of the course and this early of a marathon. James was there for moral support, and I had gotten encouragement from both Jane and Tom Jr. I beefed up my usual pre-marathon build-up of supplements, adding creatine and mega-vitamin C. And I got a B-12 shot at the corporate clinic to help me with the stress.

The course turned out to be a dream. The support in water stands was unusually strong. I felt the need to stop to relieve myself three times, yet I didn't worry about time, just finishing strong and registering my willingness to be part of the corporate team. My numbers were right: I was running the marathon on January 18, and it was my 18th marathon. I completed the course, looking and feeling strong, in 4 hours, 24 minutes. James somehow found me at the end. We sauntered back for me to make telephone calls to Gail, Jane and Tom Jr. Jane commented that she knew I would do well and had been chanting for me.

At the buffet for the team, I learned I had broken the corporate record and set a new record in my running time. Later, I found out I was in first place for my age category. What an affirmation for age 60 and my view of myself!

A few days after my return from Houston and just three

months into my tenure in the new job, I was told that there was "great unhappiness" in my unit and an atmosphere of "turmoil." I could feel myself screeching to a halt.

I tried to retrace my steps in my mind. I had been clear in talking about the job as an extension of what I was about at Chicago State University. I planned to build on what I had learned in my various positions in higher education, while focusing on the big picture of expanding opportunities for students who were underserved and disadvantaged.

In my anguish of realizing it was over, I wondered whether the problem was tied to my having betrayed my own values. I knew the view of the "mismatch" was much more complex.

Whatever had happened, I wasn't prepared to handle the situation alone. I contacted an attorney. He heard my panic. He was not unfamiliar with what I was experiencing. We were the same age, and he lost no time before bringing that up. I was hearing it again: "You're 60, and you gotta look at folding the tent." I wondered if my age had been a factor. "Why spend the time working it out when the 'old girl' just has a few more years to go?" I had not been open in celebrating being 60, and I couldn't help but think I was being put to pasture.

I began to fear that I had done something really wrong, something that was not apparent to me, but wrong in the corporate culture. But what could I have done in a mere three months? I brooded about the impact of my own transition on everyone. Had I been too rushed? Maybe I seemed burned out from trying to tie things up at CSU, manage after my mother's death, make the move and then train for both the November and January marathon? I went into denial and kept working. Kept moving ahead, knowing that I had to be prepared to move away.

I felt a sense of irony that so much of this was happening during Black History Month. "What do you have in mind for women's month?" I thought. My attorney kept me on track in assessing my options and appealing to my sense of humor. "How would you feel if you couldn't work and continue to

define your life in your career?" I asked him. I realized he did-
n't fully know what the events meant to me as a woman and as
a black woman. The very thought of leaving was unbearable.
No one has the right to define or declare for me or anyone else
when the race is over.

But here it was. Finally. I was hitting the wall and I had to
get through it. I felt embarrassed, unable to hide it and having
to face it. It was the wrong job, a mismatch. They were right.
I woke up at night with my head pounding, feeling a sense of
panic and wondering how I would get through the day. I went
into the office as if nothing had happened, upbeat in denial. I
did not tell people I was planning to resign. The staff was confused as I often shifted directions. I began to worry that my
"not working out" would indeed become a self-fulfilling
prophecy.

Where did I go wrong? I did not check out the course
thoroughly enough. I just assumed that my values matched
what they were looking for. While I could see that the corporate culture was different from what I had grown used to, I had
not looked to see if there was a coach to get me through. I
began to see the strain on my face. When I looked in the mirror, I saw the expression, the pain, I had seen in my mother's
face when she had broken down, when she had not fit in, when
she too had been different in her passion and perspective. I
was feeling older, more and more like my mother. I felt less like
running, yet I persisted and refused to surrender. I felt at times
deeply depressed. Why go on? I asked myself more than once.

I called Jane, and she reminded me to get out there and
run. "Don't surrender your power, Mom. I need you to get
through this. You can't leave it for me to deal with. Look,
Mom, you felt Grandma wanted you to take the job. Maybe
she wanted you to stand up and get through it as she had
failed to do herself."

Okay, I told myself, what matters most? Students and
improving their opportunities for success. This was my role,
my job, my life's work. I didn't want the race to be over; I did-
n't want to falter. I didn't want to run in place. I didn't want

to have to stop. I needed new ground appearing under my feet with each step. What is life without the course, the movement and going the distance? Each day I felt an emptiness that seemed to deepen when I failed to go for a literal run. My body had been part of my going the distance, but I felt estranged. I took melatonin to sleep deep sleeps and awakened at times refreshed for the course, yet there was none and the emptiness veiled me again. I sought therapy and dealt again with depression that seemed incurable by running.

My therapist prescribed Prozac and shared an article with me about a runner who had gone through a similar ordeal. I took the Prozac to renew my interest in running and stimulate my interest in my life.

Slowly, I began to fill the emptiness with running again. I looked to Jane to guide me out of the haze as she had during the divorce years ago. I implored James to be my prince. But he couldn't be everything I needed. I made frantic calls to friends to nominate me for this job or that. I did, after all, have a track record, a fact that was laden with irony.

When anyone asked me how I was, I said, "Scared and angry." Unanchored, frightened, I made projects of constantly rearranging furniture in my New York City apartment and buying clothes compulsively. The fear did not leave me.

I openly began to wonder what my whole life had been about. Did it have any meaning? What have I taught? What have I learned? While my sister reminded me that I didn't have to prove anything to anyone.

James and I went to Las Vegas for my birthday. Our plan was to engross ourselves in the slot machines and have fun, or as he would say, "Forget all the bullshit." The evening before my birthday, I began to think about what it meant that he hadn't given me a gift. I awoke and wrote out my thoughts. By morning, I had slipped into a dark mood and went out for a run along the Nevada strip before the sun was high. As I ran, the pavement started heating up, making the air shimmer. I was moving in the sunlight but there was no exhilaration, no joy, at all. I ran to the track at the University of Nevada, Las

Vegas, intent on enduring the pace for an hour, moving, navigating, determined and self-absorbed in a spiritless salute to my years on this planet. I ran hard, tasted my sweat and poured the last of my water down my back. I returned without a word to our room, aware of the impact of my mood on James. I was in a funk. But I felt I had good reason to be upset and I maintained my silence mercilessly, fueled by the flowers that Jane had thought to send. After hours of no words, my depression began to lift. We went to dinner. I apologized for my behavior. He responded by saying he accepted my apology, but he hadn't healed. He couldn't bear my mood swings; they weren't fair to him. I retreated, injured, silent again. "Why are you so angry?" he asked. "You have to find out, Dolores." I repeated the litany of things that had happened to me over the past few months, feeling that he should understand. The disappointment of things not working out. The loss of my momentum. Confusion, despair, embarrassment, rejection and vulnerability. Yet I kept hearing, "Why are you so angry?"

I stretched across the bed, and new words gave expression to my feelings. I was angry at having been left alone as my mother went to work. I was angry at having been told I had to play alone and be without other children. I was angry at my aloneness—not loneliness—but being able to count only on myself. I felt aloneness as a stutterer, the aloneness of someone who didn't quite fit in, the aloneness of being evicted. I was angry about the aloneness I felt in my young marriage. In Lakeview, my aloneness found a purpose, giving and growing. In going from one location to the next, from one challenge to another, from one level to another, I had stayed the course, moving one foot and then another, staying ahead, not looking back. Yet here I was, finally reflecting on all that forward motion. I heard myself say I am angry because I am alone. I am angry that in each new role I have become more alone. My absorption in my jobs got in the way of spending more time with my mother. I lost time with my children, leaving them alone as I pursued matters of consequence. I had been careless with friendships, my marriage, and relationships that had promise. There had always been a schedule and an agenda to master. I am angry because I am alone and have always been alone, I said.

And I am anxious that I have not taken the time to determine the cause of the post-menopausal bleeding that interrupts my routine more and more frequently as I choose to self-regulate my estrogen intake. I liken it to a "runner's injury" in a game I play with my heart and not my head. I'm so busy, moving ahead. I'm angry and pleading: "Body, spirit, don't fail me now." James listened and held me.

Jane was firm in advising me to continue the therapy. "Don't go off into the night without having your issues resolved," she said. "These are issues of your worth, your contribution and ultimately, your values. Mom, you have to be strong and take care of yourself, love yourself and reach out to help from others." Tom Jr used humor to make his point. "Mom, does this mean you'll fill all your time getting Jane and me on track? That's not for you. You're too strong a marathon-er."

I called on Gail. We talked over the phone about moving ahead. "Dolores, get into some cross-training, cycling, weights. Back off from long runs but don't stop," she said. "Let's build up for our next marathon. Want to do Portland this year?"

Getting through the wall meant confronting the truth that the course you take must match your values. I would move on. I had been perceived as not having responded to coaching, not fitting in and being too big a fish for a little pond. Yet I had entered a situation with values, come in as a strong black woman, experienced and committed to using my network to establish links among corporate mentors, pre-college programs, colleges and community groups to serve future students and communities better. My approach was bold; it required a re-examination of efforts. The response to me suggested that they had misinterpreted my quiet demeanor and perhaps expected me to be decorative and on hand to roll their initiatives.

It was clear that I had failed to set up their expectations and check the course, a pattern of behavior I had seen my mother fall into so often. Losing her, I realized, had caused me to disconnect from some of my own survival instincts. In the end, I knew I had to do what gave me energy, what tapped into my strengths, what spoke to my passion. I was not stopping. I would not be stopped.

In June, I formally resigned as head of the foundation and accepted the position of Distinguished Professor in Leadership and Diversity at the CUNY Graduate School. The decision led to a series of moves as I sent furniture to Manhattan, Chicago and Jane's house in Penbroke Pines, Florida.

It was the second summer in a row of moving. I took to saying my new mantra, "I am a black woman in my sixties and a veteran marathoner." This was a proud statement. I resisted the pathetic image of being abandoned, unconnected and alone.

Yet I was not rushing to explain anything further. The news release on my new job quoted me as saying, "It's been important to me to work for one of the country's best companies and to be a part of the foundation. I have had the opportunity to assess what matters most to me, and being the Distinguished Professor at the CUNY Graduate School best matches my interest and priorities at this time."

MILE 26.02

The wall can appear at any time, for anyone. Only you can break through the wall and find what's on the other side.

My writing became means to get through the wall, because it gave me an awareness of having established my base and achieved personal best on my way to completing my story. I worked at Sylvia Beach House on the Oregon coast, where I was encouraged by my friend and its proprietor to continue as I had done to "match my role with my person." While there, I traveled to Corvallis, Oregon, to visit Gail. We talked of the four marathons we had run together as well as the 24-hour Hood-to-Coast Relay in Oregon. I spoke of the direction of the book and its focus on going the distance. To her thinking, I was at mile 20 of a marathon and in need of getting through the wall. She cautioned me not to let the mile markers or decades of my life define the end, but rather to be guided by spirit. I returned to Manhattan to continue my running and the work on this story. After a five-mile run on the East River path, between 23rd Street and the Brooklyn Bridge, I ran to my apartment in Peter Cooper Village. I passed an older woman pushing her oxygen tank and walker. She was smartly dressed, erect and confident that she could get wherever she was going. I ran past her and then doubled back. "Way to go, stay strong," I said. She smiled and confided that she had walked to church. I wanted to say more. She was an elder, a woman teaching, learning and, most of all doing her best to get where she needed to go. Centuries of women and men have been doing this, moving past challenges and burdens to achieve all they are capable of achieving. I ran on.

It had been 20 years since I had been to CUNY as vice chancellor for student affairs and special programs. I met with Edith and Henry Everett to learn of the CUNY of 1998. Edith, a trustee, had chaired the search committee that had hired me for the post. We had stayed in touch throughout the years and I was buoyed by her gutsy approach to issues of access and her commitment to help the underserved. We spoke of how the late Chancellor Robert Kibbee would have been disappointed to see how things had turned around. There were many on the current Board of Trustees who questioned the university's investment in remedial education and support for students who had been underserved yet had potential and determination to succeed. Those of us who were committed to certain values had to stay strong and focused, we agreed. They doubted, and I tended to agree, that I would enjoy the "good life" as a professor. I shared how I often awakened in the middle of the night, restless for something more. With no department assignment and having been given the freedom to initiate and implement a seminar series and do my own research, I felt unconnected. Yet in the midst of my feeling adrift, colleagues were nominating me for college presidencies.

I found myself involved in final discussions with a search committee for the president of Morris Brown College in Atlanta. But I wasn't sure. I consulted my friend and colleague Grant Venerable, former associate provost at CSU. Over dinner one night, he and I sketched out not only the meaning of this opportunity but the multitude of ways in which I could help Morris Brown and its 2,000 students. Founded by slaves, the 114-year-old historically black liberal arts college is one of the pillars of the Atlanta University (AU) Center, along with Clark-Atlanta University, Morehouse and Spelman Colleges, Interdenominational Theological Seminary and Morehouse Medical School. The AU occupies hallowed ground in African-American educational and church history, having been home to significant leaders and scholars, from W.E.B. Du Bois to John Hope Franklin, Howard Thurman, Benjamin Mays and Martin Luther King Jr. I wondered if I could provide the leadership this Southern black institution needed to overcome both enormous economic and cultural challenges.

Once I visited the College and met the students, however,

I felt connected. The campus was divided by Martin Luther King Jr. Boulevard. I stood on the bridge that I had seen in photographs of King's funeral. It had been crowded with people as his casket passed. I visited the Du Bois room, where Du Bois wrote and lectured. I began to visualize the campus with more flowers, more trees and greater energy. By the end of my visit, I knew I would say yes to the job.

By November 1998, I was managing graduate seminars at CUNY and working to stay on top of my e-mail communications as chair of the American Association of Higher Education, vice chair of Campus Compact and a member of many other organizations. And I was handling the transition to the day-to-day duties at Morris Brown.

My step was lighter and quicker. Living my life in tune with what mattered most to me made the wall recede into memory as an obstacle met and overcome. James saw me as needing time to heal but I felt that my forward motion was healing. We compromised with a three-week vacation in Rio Caliente, Mexico, where there was time to vacation, complete the first draft of manuscript and celebrate the new year.

I approached the job at Morris Brown College with a plan for success. I would hire an experienced, focused team of senior managers, build the office of institutional advancement and project a vision based on an understanding of our students and their realities before, during and after their experiences at Morris Brown. I would implement the vision with an understanding of the institution and how its academic integrity, its fiscal integrity, and the quality of its infrastructure were inseparably linked. And I would share, communicate, market and implement the vision with deliberation. To do these things, I would take risks, act, be accountable and, most important for me, I would stay in touch with my body and spirit.

I had no illusions that the job would be easy. When I shared the news with Peter Drucker, he responded that President Clinton should send me to Kosovo, given my passion for challenges.

I would be the first female president of Morris Brown

College. I had never lived for an extended period in the South nor had I attended an historically black college or university. Furthermore, I am Baptist, not AME. What I offered was a passion to help students with the potential and determination to succeed. These students shared a commitment to service. They were convinced that getting an education would adequately prepare them for graduate school or a career.

To signal stability for the college community and delineate a point of reassessment for me as well as the trustees, I signed a contract that would take me through the 2001 academic year. I decided not to let the college invest its slim resources in building a president's house but to use those funds instead to refurbish a residence hall for our students. And I urged the trustees to boost their level of contributions by making a $10,000 donation to the school.

As president of Morris Brown, I knew that I had arrived at a point where I was now confident and sure of "doing it right." The experiences of many years and the processes that had been a part of me for so long were, at last, being put in place. The next steps seemed to flow from there.

The vision that I created—the Learning Tree—was in line with the historic mission of the college and with my commitment to "putting students first." Just as in a race, I knew that the level of urgency had to be raised. I insisted on honest discussion, allowing errors to blow up. I asked for relevant data, such as monthly reports from my Executive Council. These reports had to fit in with the way that I wanted to run the college, not with the way textbooks might define the role of a leader. We all had to "walk the talk" and abide by the values of the vision. These were times that led to crisis, but crisis afforded an opportunity to share information and build an effective team, one that was based on trust and a common goal, one that was ready to understand Morris Brown and its students.

As I worked with people to implement the Learning Tree vision, I realized more and more that my kind of leadership was different from the norm. To me, it was clear that my

notions of "jumping the curve" and "walking the talk" of innovation and strategic choices were far from linear. I had come
to trust my own intuition and experience as well as my heart
and passion. My doing "the next right thing," keeping options
open, seeking new resources aggressively and making intelligent, informed decisions as opportunities appeared represented an evolutionary way of planning and acting. True, this was
sometimes an imperfect process, but it was always based on
pragmatic solutions, flexibility and deeply held values about
the need for all of us to be of service to students.

In my Founder's Day speech a few months after beginning at Morris Brown, I spoke of going the distance. "As a distance runner, I have experienced the exhilaration of being in
the fray, buoyed by the proper training and having established
a base, and proceeding with the confidence that comes from
being in tune with my body. You must pump your arms,
breathe evenly, begin the race strong, maintain a pace, move
ahead and remain focused on what you must achieve," I told
the audience. I spoke as well of the college being at a cross-
roads, one not much different from my own. "This is a defining moment. Those of us who love the college must act deci-
sively and we must act now! I can provide the leadership, and
I am willing to go the distance. But can we get there? Can we
achieve our goal?" "Consider your power," I said. "The race
is just beginning. We're in it, doing our personal best, rooted
in our beliefs. I ask you to go the distance."

A few weeks after that talk, I ran the U.S. American Track
and Field Southeastern Regional Masters 5K race sponsored by
the Atlanta Track Club. What a joy to be in a race in that soft
Atlanta spring! Shortly after I completed the race, full of the
satisfaction of having run well, I got a call at home from Julia
Emmens, the executive director.

"Dolores, when the results were graded for age, you
placed in the top three!" That made me smile.

I smiled even more later that spring when 1,196
students—from sixth graders to high school seniors—joined us
in a seven-month pre-college program. After that program, fall

1999 enrollment at Morris Brown was up 13.5 percent—a personal best for the college and a great accomplishment for all the students who now have an opportunity to achieve at the college level. As the school song goes, "I'm so glad I'm at Morris Brown."

AFTERWORD

Relax. Release. Relate. Re-invent. My rhythm continues to evolve with each new race.

Yㅇou have run long and hard. Your muscles ache, yet you feel that if you have to, you can go farther. You're feeling proud and strong. You understand your past. You know how to stay focused and resourceful. You're feeling much younger than your 60-plus years and not at all comfortable with any suggestion that you have peaked.

When associates the same age or older start sentences with, "When you get to be our age," and then go on to list all the restrictions on movement, sex, lifestyle and relationships, you just have to remember your early morning run or plan your next marathon. Your clock does not have to tick as loudly as theirs.

The clock starts early. Women friends in their 30s and 40s struggle to face "having it all." They think about their time left and where they want to be at 50, at 60. Baby boomers have such concerns about facing their empty nests, losing all the vestiges of their youth.

For me, at 60, the questions are different and my footsteps have rendered my clock almost inaudible. I worry instead about why the term "graying of America" implies the "decaying of America." I wonder why my peers don't scream out what they have achieved when there is a suggestion that their history is meaningless, a blank page. I wonder what will happen if younger people don't become more politically involved to solve the problems of homelessness, disadvantage and poverty. The distance continues to beckon. The race is not over.

My daughter Jane wrote the following poem on my running of the 100th Marathon in Boston in April 1996.

Going the Distance
To Mom, the woman with life legs of steel

Starting with
The banner of
Your birth
You took a
Swift step
Forward and
Another until
You found
Yourself airborne
With feet in
Flight
Charging past
An environment
Of particular
Persons, places
And things
To move sweetly
Into the sky
Air pushes
Forward to
Let you pass
It,
As you drench
Yourself in
Water,
Push your legs
Of the earth,
And blaze a
Trail of fire,
You run with
The elements of
Life and
Your life is
In its element

For it is
Finding ways
To scorch a
Path which
Will burn
Brightly long
After the
Running is
Done.
There is nothing
Upon which
You tread
Lightly.
Your falling
Feet hitting
Unyielding
Pavement
Again
And
Again
And
Again
A
Trillion
Times
Are protected
As they
Lurch forever
Forward by
The padding
And depth
Of the soles
Of your soul
As you run
The marathon
Of life,
You realize

That we
Choose our
Own finish
Lines by
How
We run the
Course of
The race.
You know
That there
Is always
A first place
Waiting to
Be won
If we choose,
If we are
Prepared
To go
The Distance...

Jane E. Cross

Appendix

MARATHON TRAINING PROGRAM

My training program includes a vigorous 16-week marathon preparation schedule. Divided into three stages of 4 weeks, 4 weeks, and 8 weeks, the schedule calls for increasing intensity in my runs and workouts. I build from 20 to 43 miles a week and increase my hard workouts from one to three. I also work with weights according to the weights/aerobics videotape put out by The FIRM. The plan that follows is the one I use. Gail Vanderheide, my running partner and a middle school teacher, helped me develop this regimen to, as she puts it, "get the job done with minimum effort and time investment."

WEIGHTS

I used to use small free weights and a program from *Runner's World* magazine. Now I use 3 lb., 5 lb. and 8 lb. weights and The FIRM videotaped weight workout with aerobics. I like the convenience and toning and posture benefits. The workouts strengthen me over the hills and fortify my quads so that I am in much better shape for miles 20-26.

OFF WEEKS

I build "off weeks" into the training to allow for travel or sometimes for just a week of being under the weather. The off weeks can be written in and taken as needed. It relieves the guilt I feel when I just have to get a long run done and circumstances prevent it. I always start with good intentions to not use the "off weeks," but then reality sets in. It usually isn't my lack of motivation but obligations that force me to adjust the running to fit others' plans.

HILLS

"Hills" are hard to define unless you are a climber or geologist. They can vary in length from 0.1 mile to 0.8 mile and rise as much as 400 feet. A hill run means a mile warm-up, and then up and down hills for about 4-6 more miles.

SPEED

"Speed" and "pyramids" are interchangeable. For speed I go to a track (440 yards) and run a one-mile warm up and then begin fast work. I build up from 220s to 880s but never do more than 3 miles fast. Recovery between reps varies. Sometimes I do a standing recovery or jog/walk an equal distance between reps to recover. Speeds are as follows:

> 220 = 42-46 seconds
> 440 = 1:25-1:45 seconds
> 880 = 3:15-3:30 seconds

Usually I don't do much cool down, maybe at most half a mile or twice around the track. Total distance, at most is about 5 miles. The workout takes about 1 hour. These are tough to get in when daylight is limited in late August and September.

PYRAMIDS

These are probably my favorite. I read about marathon runner Grete Waitz's workouts that included these and tried them. I warm up for 1.5-2 miles on the road. Then using a stopwatch, I run fast for 1 minute, then jog/walk for 1 minute, then run fast for 2 minutes, then jog/walk for 2 minutes, and so on, up to five minutes fast with a five-minute recovery. Then I go back down: 4 minutes fast, 4 recovery, and so on, down to 1 minute. This is a very efficient way to do speed work. It can be done almost anywhere you can find an uninterrupted space without breaks to wait for traffic. Varied terrain makes them fun. I start with a 1 min./2 min./2 min./1 min. set and add about 3 minutes per week until I'm up to a 1/2/3/4/5/4/3/2/1 set. I usually don't do much of a cool down after these either. The total distance of the longest run is about 7 miles and takes a little over 1 hour.

LONG RUNS

These start at 10 miles and build by 2 miles every other week, up to 24 miles about 2 or 3 weeks before the marathon. Pace is anywhere from an 8:45 or 9:00 mile to an 8:00 mile if I'm feeling frisky for a mile or two late in the run. I used to time these runs but now I just take a "sample" mile from old race markings on the pavement at a couple of points in the run. I try to drink water every 2-3 miles and will sometimes stop for bathroom breaks if needed.

REPEAT MILES

This is probably the run I like the least but it pays off in race results. I do them on the weekends alternating with long runs. I do fast mile repeats, on the road or highway, using highway mile markers or old race marks on the pavement. I warm up about 2 miles, then start. I try to keep the pace at 6:50 to 7:15 per mile. After a fast mile I do a standing recovery of 30 seconds to 2 minutes, and off I go again. I start with 2 miles fast in a 10-mile run and built up to 12 or 14 miles fast in a 16 mile run. That last one is a killer! It helps to have a friend to run these with, as they can be quite demanding.

HILL REPS

I have a set hill that takes about 1 minute to run up. It isn't so steep that it puts me on my toes, but it is a challenge. After 2 warm-up miles I go up the hill , running as fast as I can, timing the rep. These are really fun to do with buddies of about the same ability. You can take turns "chasing" each other, challenging, passing and leading. After a run up, we walk down as a recovery. I start with 3 and add one rep a week up to 8 reps at the peak of training.